LESSONS FROM MY CAREER AS A

SOFTWARE ENGINEER

IYIOLA LADEJO

Copyright © 2024 IYIOLA LADEJO

All Rights Reserved.

LESSONS FROM MY CAREER AS A SOFTWARE ENGINEER

No portion of this book may be reproduced, stored, or shared in any form—whether electronic, mechanical, photocopying, recording, or via any other retrieval system—without express written permission from the copyright holder.

This publication is intended **solely for educational and informational purposes** and does not constitute financial or professional advice.

The author and publisher make no representations or warranties regarding the completeness, accuracy, or reliability of the content and do not endorse any third-party services, products, or links referenced herein.

TABLE OF CONTENTS

INTRODUCTION

Software engineering is more than just writing code. It's a journey of continuous learning, a path marked by moments of failure, discovery, and growth. Over the years, I've realized that success in this field isn't solely about mastering new languages or frameworks, but it is about understanding the deeper principles of problem-solving, collaboration, and system design. In Lessons from My Career as a Software Engineer, I'll share the experiences, challenges, and insights that have shaped my journey, offering a window into the mindset and philosophy that have helped me grow as an engineer.

This book isn't just for seasoned developers; it's for anyone who's ever sat in front of a terminal, puzzled over a bug, or dreamed of building something meaningful. Whether you're just starting out or have been in the trenches for years, these lessons will resonate with the shared experience of being a software creator. From the mistakes that taught me the most, to the mentors who inspired me, I hope this collection of reflections provides not just technical guidance, but a deeper understanding of what it truly means to be a software engineer.

CHAPTER ONE
How Software Engineering Became My Craft

It's hard to pinpoint the exact moment when software engineering became more than just a skill for me. Like many engineers, my journey wasn't a linear one, nor did I experience a single epiphany that led me to believe that this was my true calling. Instead, it was a gradual unfolding, a series of small moments and experiences that, when we were woven together, formed the tapestry of my passion for code. If I had to describe it, I'd say it was like discovering a new language, one that spoke not only to my intellect but to a deeper part of me, something creative, challenging, and endlessly fascinating.

My first encounter with software development was, in a sense, accidental. Growing up, I wasn't one of those kids who was naturally drawn to computers, nor did I have a deep affinity for technology. I remember, in my early teens, being more interested in reading, playing sports, or sketching than in anything remotely related to the digital world. Technology was something distant, a tool I used without fully understanding how it worked. But that changed when I encountered my first programming language: QBasic.

It wasn't a class or a formal lesson that introduced me to it but it was more of a serendipitous discovery. One day, I was browsing through an old PC in my family's basement, a relic from the late '90s. My fingers danced over the keyboard as I poked around the various files, and I stumbled upon QBasic. The simple, dark interface with its blinking cursor seemed almost mysterious. I opened it, not really understanding what I was looking at, but intrigued by the presence of a blank screen and a blinking cursor waiting for commands. There was something magnetic about it. In hindsight, it wasn't the most sophisticated development environment, but it was enough to spark a curiosity that I couldn't ignore. I spent the next few weeks experimenting, copying lines of code from tutorials I found online, typing them into the console, and watching as simple text appeared on the screen or as characters moved across it in simple graphics. The first time I successfully wrote a small program something as basic as a number-guessing game, I was hooked. I could still remember the rush of excitement, the thrill of creating something that, through a few lines of code, was uniquely mine. It was as though I'd unlocked a new way to communicate with the machine, a secret language that let me bring my ideas to life.

Looking back, it wasn't just the process of writing code that intrigued me. It was the problem-solving aspect, the intellectual puzzle of it all. The feeling of starting with nothing, just a blank screen and building something functional, however simple, from scratch was intoxicating. But more than that, I discovered that coding was a way to structure my thoughts. It was like organizing chaos, a way to take the abstract and transform it into something tangible. The joy of that transformation, the beauty in the process of turning an idea into a functioning program was, to me, an entirely new form of creation.

At that point, I wasn't aware of the depth of software engineering as a discipline. For me, it was just a fascinating hobby, something I could do in my spare time, tucked away in the quiet of my room. But even in that early stage, I began to sense that this wasn't like other hobbies. There was something about it that felt more consequential, more challenging, and more rewarding. It was like a puzzle that never ended, where every time I solved one problem, a new one emerged. As I got older, I started to take coding more seriously. I realized that if I wanted to truly understand this craft, I would need to dive deeper. Secondary school computer science classes were the next step. There, I was introduced to more formal programming languages like C and Java, which felt like a leap forward compared to QBasic. The structured nature of these languages, combined with the complexity of their syntax and logic, forced me to think more critically about how to solve problems.

I'll admit, at first, I struggled. The shift from QBasic to Java was disorienting. The language felt more rigid, more formal, and the logic seemed more abstract. I encountered bugs that made no sense, errors that I couldn't debug, and concepts like memory management and recursion that completely baffled me. But rather than giving up, I pushed through the frustration. I could sense, even then, that this challenge was part of what made coding so compelling, it was the process of continuously grappling with complexity and uncertainty until, suddenly, something clicked.

What kept me going was the sense of progress. The early victories such as getting a loop to run correctly, understanding how variables interact, or figuring out how to structure a simple program were small, but they were real. With each small success, I felt a sense of accomplishment that made the next challenge more exciting. The process itself, the grind of debugging and problem-solving, became addictive. Each mistake was a lesson, and each solution felt like a step closer to mastery.

As I moved on to college and began to formally study science, my passion for code only deepened. I was introduced to more advanced concepts like algorithms, data structures, and software architecture. But even more important than the technical knowledge I gained was the realization that coding was not just a means to an end. It was a mindset, a way of thinking about the world.

I began to view problems not just as challenges to overcome, but as systems to understand. The world of software development was, to me, a beautiful abstraction of reality. Every application, every program, every system was a set of interwoven components working together in harmony. Understanding these systems, how to optimize them, and how to design them to scale, was what truly fascinated me. In a way, software engineering became a lens through which I viewed everything else which is problem-solving in life, communication, even creativity itself. Code became my tool to shape the world, not just in terms of software, but in a broader sense, as a way of organizing and structuring complex ideas.

What I didn't realize then was that this early fascination would ultimately shape my entire career. Like many in the field, I started out coding for the sheer joy of it. I didn't know where it would lead me or what impact it would have on my life. But looking back, I can see now that those formative moments such as the first time I wrote a program in QBasic, the struggles with Java, and the late nights spent debugging were the moments that ignited a passion that has only grown stronger over time. In the beginning, my relationship with code was like a first love, intense, consuming, and full of wonder. As I gained more experience, that love matured into a deeper, more thoughtful relationship. Coding became less about the rush of creation and more about the responsibility of crafting something meaningful. But even now, years later, I still feel that same spark, the excitement of solving a problem, the joy of making something that works, and the satisfaction of knowing that, through code, I can have a real impact.

And if there's one lesson, I would want others to take away from this, it's that passion for coding doesn't always strike in the obvious ways. It doesn't have to be love at first sight. For me, it was a slow burn, an evolving relationship that grew stronger with every challenge, every mistake, and every breakthrough. But once it caught fire, it never went out.

Now, I have said that in the early days of my journey as a software engineer, the focus was clear: get the code to work. I was driven by the desire to make things functional, to see the programs I wrote come to life, whether that meant a simple "Hello, World!" message or a small game that ran without errors. Success was measured by how quickly I could make something work, how fast I could learn a new syntax, or how efficiently I could fix a bug. I was focused on the immediate, tangible results such as the thrill of the first successful compile, the rush of solving a problem, the joy of seeing a program do what I told it to do.

But, as with all things in life, the deeper I ventured into the world of software engineering, the more I began to realize that simply getting the code to work wasn't enough. I had learned the hard way that functionality alone didn't guarantee quality. While building applications that functioned was the first milestone in my growth as an engineer, it was not the end of the journey, it was only the beginning.

As my career progressed, I found myself drawn into more complex projects, ones that demanded not just functionality, but reliability, scalability, and maintainability. The thrill of solving a problem for the first time was still there, but it became apparent that code, like any form of creation, required more than just the ability to solve problems.

It required care, craftsmanship, and a deep understanding of the systems you were building. Over time, I began to shift my focus from simply writing code to thinking about the broader implications of the software I was creating. This shift was not instantaneous; it was gradual, as I learned from both my successes and my failures.

I remember the first time I worked on a large-scale project that required collaboration with other developers. It was a simple web application, nothing groundbreaking, just a straightforward tool for managing user data. At the time, I had been working on small personal projects, where the structure of the codebase was entirely under my control. There was no need to think about how my code would interact with others. But this project was different. It wasn't just my code; it was part of a larger system, one that had to scale, be maintainable, and fit into the team's workflow. The first time I encountered a pull request in a collaborative setting, I was floored. I had to adapt not just to the code, but to a new way of thinking about software development. This was where I started to realize that creating software was more than just coding but it was about designing systems that would work, not just today, but in the future as well.

It was during this period that I started learning the importance of clean code. Initially, my code was functional, but messy. It worked, but it was often hard to read, hard to maintain, and difficult to scale. I didn't realize it at the time, but I was already encountering the first signs of what would later become one of the most important aspects of software engineering: craftsmanship. I began to read books which opened my eyes to a new world of best practices, patterns, and principles. I learned that writing clean, well-structured code was as much about the process of writing as it was about the final product.

The realization that writing code could be a form of craftsmanship, something akin to an art form, was a revelation. It wasn't enough to just get the code to run. I had to think about how to make it readable, how to make it maintainable, how to ensure it could be scaled and adapted in the future. I learned to ask myself questions like: Can someone else understand this code? Is this the best possible way to solve this problem? How can I refactor this to make it cleaner, faster, and more modular? I began to see the value in naming variables meaningfully, writing modular functions, and adhering to design patterns that made my code not just functional, but elegant and efficient.

One of the most significant shifts in my growth from coder to craftsman was the realization that programming was not just about solving the problem at hand, but it also involved anticipating future problems and creating code that could adapt and grow with time. I started to think beyond the immediate task and consider how my code would evolve over the next few months or years. Would it be easy to add new features? Would someone else be able to work on it? Would it be easy to debug? These were the questions I hadn't considered in my early days, when I was just getting the code to work. Now, they have become central to my approach.

As I gained more experience, I encountered projects where these principles were put to the test. One of the most formative experiences in this regard was working on a long-term, multi-phase project for a client. This was not a short-term sprint, but a year-long endeavor with changing requirements, changing deadlines, and a growing team. The challenges I faced were not just technical, but logistical. How could we design a system that would remain flexible in the face of constantly changing demands? How could we ensure that new features wouldn't break existing functionality? How could we keep the codebase clean, even as it grew larger and more complex? The experience taught me that creating software wasn't just about solving a series of problems, but it was about managing complexity. As the project progressed, I learned how to design systems that were both resilient and adaptable, keeping the long-term health of the project in mind.

One of the key lessons I took from this project was the importance of writing tests. In the early days, I didn't fully appreciate the role that testing played in software development. Tests, to me, were an afterthought more like a chore that could be skipped if I was in a rush or too focused on finishing a feature. But as the project grew more complex, I began to see the value of having a solid testing framework in place. Unit tests, integration tests, and end-to-end tests became the safety net that allowed us to move quickly and confidently, knowing that we had checks in place to catch regressions and bugs before they made it into production. Writing tests was no longer an afterthought; it became an integral part of my development process.

Another important aspect of my growth was learning how to work effectively in teams. Early on, I had been used to working on small, personal projects where I was the sole developer. But as I entered more professional environments, I realized that collaboration was an essential skill for any software engineer. I learned to communicate effectively with colleagues, share knowledge, and contribute to group discussions. I learned to give and receive feedback, whether it was in the form of a code review or a design critique. Collaboration wasn't just about getting the job done but was about making the team's collective knowledge and skills greater than the sum of its parts. I came to realize that no matter how skilled I was, the best software was always the product of a collaborative effort. I will touch more of these in future chapters.

Craftsmanship in software engineering is about taking pride in what you build, not just in the outcome but in the process. It's about continually striving for improvement, learning from mistakes, and always pushing yourself to do better. Craftsmanship is a mindset that values quality over speed, elegance over quick fixes, and long-term solutions over short-term patches. It's about creating software that is not just functional, but a joy to work with both for the developer writing it and for the users who rely on it.

Looking back on my journey, it's clear to me now that the transition from code to craft didn't happen overnight. It was a gradual process, shaped by both successes and failures, by moments of frustration and moments of clarity. But through it all, the goal was always the same:

to create software that not only worked but worked well. To create software that was more than just a solution to a problem but was a piece of craftsmanship, something I could be proud of. And while I'm still far from perfect, I've come to appreciate the journey itself. The learning never stops, and that, to me, is the beauty of software engineering. There's always room to grow, always something new to learn, and always a new way to improve. As I continue to hone my craft, I realize that the evolution from code to craft isn't a destination, it's a lifelong process. But it's a process that I wouldn't trade for anything. After all, what could be more rewarding than creating something that, at its best, can change the world?

The place of having a solid philosophy and mindset is pivotal in achieving the very best in this profession. The satisfaction of solving a problem was the driving force behind my work. But over time, as I progressed in my career, I began to realize that software engineering was not just about creating solutions or writing code, but it was a philosophy, a way of thinking about the world. This realization didn't come all at once, but rather over the course of years, as I faced challenges, learned from mistakes, and encountered ideas and experiences that forced me to rethink what it meant to be a software engineer.

At the core of this philosophical shift was the understanding that software engineering, like any craft, requires a lifelong commitment to learning, evolving, and adapting. It's easy, especially early in one's career, to view programming as a technical skill or a tool to be mastered, a means to an end. But as I gained experience, I saw that software engineering is more than just a skill set; it's a mindset, a philosophy that guides how we approach problems, how we think about technology, and how we relate to the ever-changing world around us.

The first sign of this philosophical shift came when I realized that the best engineers were not necessarily those who knew the most programming languages or had the most technical expertise. Rather, they were the ones who embraced the idea of lifelong learning. As technology evolves, new languages, frameworks, and tools emerge. The tools we use to build software today will likely be obsolete in a few years, but the mindset of a lifelong learner which is the willingness to adapt, to evolve, and to grow is timeless. This philosophy of continuous improvement became a cornerstone of my approach to software engineering.

In the early years, I was eager to solve problems quickly, to finish projects and move on to the next challenge. I believed that the mark of a good software engineer was the ability to solve complex problems, often under pressure, and to write code that worked. But over time, I came to understand that solving a problem quickly didn't always mean solving it well. I began to realize that the true measure of an engineer's skill lies not in their ability to solve a problem once, but in their ability to solve problems over time, consistently, effectively, and with a mindset that takes into account long-term maintainability, scalability, and adaptability.

This shift in thinking led me to embrace the idea of sustainable software development. In the past, I had worked on projects with an eye to getting things done as quickly as possible. The code had to work, the deadlines had to be met, and I was driven by the excitement of delivering a functional product. But as I advanced in my career, I started to see that speed and functionality were not the only measures of success. A sustainable solution wasn't just one that worked now; it was one that could continue to work as it evolved, one that was built to adapt, scale, and grow with time. The best code I learned was code that stood the test of time not just because it functioned well today, but because it could easily evolve as requirements changed, as new features were added, and as new developers joined the team.

As I developed this mindset, I also began to reflect on the impact of software on the world. Early in my career, I focused mostly on solving problems in isolation, fixing bugs, optimizing code, or building new features. But over time, I started to see the bigger picture: the software we build doesn't exist in a vacuum. It impacts people's lives, whether directly or indirectly. Every line of code I write has the potential to affect users, businesses, and even society at large. With this realization, I began to approach software development not just as a technical exercise, but as a moral and ethical responsibility. How could I ensure that the systems I built were accessible, user-friendly, and fair? How could I ensure that the software I created would help people rather than harm them?

One pivotal moment in my career that shaped this mindset came when I worked on a project involving financial technology, an application that was used by thousands of people to manage their personal finances. I was responsible for building a feature that allowed users to track their spending and set budgets. As I worked on the project, I was struck by the profound impact that the software could have on users' lives. It wasn't just about writing code to track transactions but was about giving people the tools to make better financial decisions, to improve their lives. This made me think about the ethical implications of what I was building. I began to see software engineering not just as a technical challenge but as a moral one. How could I build systems that were transparent, secure, and respectful of users' privacy? How could I design systems that didn't just serve business goals but also contributed positively to society?

I became more aware of the ethical dimensions of software engineering; I also began to think about the broader social responsibility of engineers. We have the power to build systems that can change the way people live, work, and communicate. But with that power comes responsibility. The software we create can have far-reaching consequences. We've seen how algorithms can amplify biases, how poorly designed systems can lead to inefficiency or inequality, and how technology can sometimes outpace our understanding of its impact. With every line of code we write, we must ask ourselves: How will this affect people? Is this solution fair? Is it ethical?

In my later years, I found myself mentoring younger engineers, guiding them through their own journeys. This was an experience that deepened my philosophy of software engineering. I realized that mentorship was not just about teaching technical skills but was about helping them develop the ability to think critically, to approach problems from multiple angles, and to understand the broader context in which software is created. It was about fostering an environment where curiosity, humility, and a passion for learning could flourish. As I guided others through their challenges, I also found that teaching reinforced my own understanding of the principles and philosophies that had shaped my career. Mentorship became a way for me to share not just knowledge, but the values that had helped me grow as an engineer.

One of the most important lessons I imparted to my mentees was the importance of reflection. Early in my career, I was focused on getting things done on pushing through the code, meeting deadlines, and shipping features. But over time, I realized that reflection is an essential part of growth. Taking time to look back on what went well, what didn't, and what could have been done better is crucial to improving as an engineer. Reflection helps us understand the bigger picture and allows us to learn from our experiences, both good and bad. It's easy to get caught up in the day-to-day hustle of writing code, but without reflection, we risk repeating the same mistakes and missing opportunities for growth.

The philosophy of software engineering that I developed over the years is one of continuous learning, collaboration, and ethical responsibility. It's about viewing software not just as a product, but as a practice, an evolving craft that requires ongoing dedication, reflection, and care.

CHAPTER TWO
The Art of Debugging: Patience, Precision and Perseverance

Software engineering, despite its deep technical roots, is as much about mindset as it is about skill. Few activities in programming expose this truth as much as debugging. Debugging is not simply a task that needs to be completed but it's a mental and emotional journey that demands more than technical know-how. It requires a unique mindset, one that blends patience, perseverance, and precision. In fact, debugging is as much about managing your emotions and approaching problem-solving as it is about identifying the root cause of an issue in the codebase.

For many engineers, the first encounter with debugging comes as a frustrating and perplexing experience. When a bug emerges, especially in a complex system, it can feel like an overwhelming obstacle. The code isn't doing what you expect it to, and every step toward fixing it seems to open a new can of worms. In those moments, when your patience is wearing thin and frustration threatens to take over, the true nature of debugging emerges. Debugging is not just about solving problems and is about solving them thoughtfully, with resilience and a mindset that embraces the process of discovery. This mindset doesn't come naturally; it needs to be cultivated and nurtured through experience, practice, and reflection.

The heart of debugging lies a paradox. Debugging is, by nature, a process filled with uncertainty. You don't always know what's causing the issue, and every step you take could lead you in the wrong direction. This uncertainty breeds frustration. The emotional experience of debugging is something every seasoned engineer can relate to. When I first started out, I had no idea how to navigate these feelings. Every bug felt like a personal failure. If I couldn't get my code to work, I felt like I had failed, even though the truth is far more nuanced. As I encountered more bugs, I started to realize that debugging wasn't about eliminating failure but learning how to deal with it constructively.

In the early stages of my career, encountering a bug felt like a defeat. I'd pour over lines of code, expecting a quick resolution, only to find that the problem was deeper than anticipated, or more elusive than I imagined. Each failed attempt to solve the issue would chip away at my confidence. The process was not linear. Sometimes I'd get lucky and find the solution after just a few tries. But more often, I'd be caught in a cycle of frustration, moving in circles, running into dead ends, and feeling the weight of the problem bearing down on me. It's easy to give in to this frustration, but as I grew as an engineer, I learned that debugging is a test of resilience. You cannot rush the process, nor can you expect a magical solution to emerge immediately. The bug will reveal itself when the time is right.

In those early years, I found that patience was the most important thing I could cultivate. It wasn't just patience in terms of the hours spent debugging (though that's certainly a factor); it was patience with myself, my process, and my expectations. Debugging requires a mindset that is comfortable with ambiguity. If you're unable to embrace the uncertainty that comes with debugging, then you risk getting stuck in an emotional loop of frustration. Patience isn't just about waiting for a bug to resolve itself but about navigating that emotional rollercoaster with a sense of calm and control.

It's easy to think of patience as passive as a kind of waiting for the solution to present itself, like watching water boil. But when it comes to debugging, patience must be active. It's not about sitting idly and hoping the answer will emerge. It's about knowing that the solution is out there and committing to the iterative process of finding it. Debugging teaches you how to focus, how to zoom in on the small details without getting distracted, how to isolate potential causes of failure, and how to patiently test theories without jumping to conclusions.

The key to developing this kind of focused patience is to embrace the iterative nature of debugging. Early on, I would often try to jump to conclusions too quickly, assuming I knew what the bug was based on limited information. This mindset, fueled by impatience, was more likely to lead me astray than to find the solution. I'd assume the problem was a simple syntax error, or a minor logical mistake, and race to fix it. But as I encountered more complex bugs, I learned that jumping ahead without understanding the problem would only waste time in the long run.

I began to slow down. I would step back from the code, take a deep breath, and focus on observing the system's behavior carefully. I learned to ask myself key questions: What exactly is going wrong? What did I expect to happen? What happens when I make this change? How is the system behaving now? By taking a step back, I could approach the problem with greater clarity and focus. Rather than rushing to fix something, I now focused on understanding it, on isolating the issue and observing every small change that occurred as I tested different fixes. This patience allowed me to dig deeper into the problem, explore different possibilities, and eventually uncover the root cause. In many ways, debugging is like solving a puzzle. It requires patience to examine every piece, test every hypothesis, and connect the dots. As I gained experience, I began to see that a good debugger is someone who is comfortable with uncertainty and able to maintain a clear, focused mindset. Debugging is not about finding a quick fix but it's about carefully peeling back the layers of the system until the problem reveals itself. It's an active patience, one that is driven by curiosity, observation, and methodical testing.

The key to navigating the frustrating moments of debugging lies in reframing frustration itself. Frustration is often seen as a negative emotion, something to be avoided. But in debugging, frustration becomes a powerful tool for understanding the problem at hand. The feeling of being stuck is actually an indicator that something needs to change in your approach. It's a reminder that the solution isn't obvious yet, but that doesn't mean it's unreachable. It's in these moments of frustration that your patience and persistence are truly tested.

One memorable experience from early in my career illustrates this point. I was working on a particularly tricky bug that had eluded me for days. The application was crashing intermittently, and no amount of logging or testing seemed to catch the issue. I was convinced that the problem was in one part of the code, but no matter how many changes I made, the crash persisted. After days of chasing my tail, I found myself staring at the screen, feeling utterly defeated. In that moment of frustration, I took a break, walked away from the code, and gave myself some space.

When I returned, I approached the problem with fresh eyes. I stopped looking for a quick fix and instead tried to understand the system as a whole. By testing the system's behavior in various configurations and combinations, I finally discovered the issue: a rare edge case I hadn't considered. The frustration, rather than a sign of failure, had pushed me to step back and approach the problem from a new perspective. In hindsight, I realized that it was my patience and taking the time to reset and return with a clear mind that had allowed me to find the solution. Frustration had become a signal to slow down, focus, and test further.

This experience reinforced a critical lesson: debugging isn't just about finding the bug. It's about learning how to navigate the emotional and mental challenges that come with it. Debugging is frustrating, but it is also deeply rewarding when we embrace the process. Every bug we fix deepens our understanding of the system, sharpens our problem-solving skills, and builds our emotional resilience.

Each debugging session is an opportunity for growth, not just in technical ability, but in emotional and cognitive maturity. Debugging teaches us how to handle uncertainty, how to maintain focus in the face of frustration, and how to persevere through failure. Every bug that is resolved adds to our toolkit of knowledge, our understanding of the system, and our mental fortitude.

The first step in any debugging process is reproducing the bug. Until you can consistently reproduce the issue, you're flying blind and attempting to address something that is either fleeting or ill-defined. Reproducing the bug allows you to observe its behavior in a controlled environment and lays the groundwork for a successful investigation. Without this, debugging becomes a guessing game; you're not working with facts, but with assumptions. Reproducing the bug is where the investigation begins, this is where the trail starts, and it's often the most important step. For many of us, the most frustrating part of debugging is trying to reproduce an error that only occurs intermittently or under specific conditions. A bug that occurs randomly or is tied to a rare set of conditions can feel elusive, almost like trying to capture smoke in your hands. But even with these elusive bugs, the key is to set up a systematic environment in which you can trigger the bug consistently. This may involve isolating parts of the system, tweaking parameters, or even replicating the environment in which the bug occurs.

Once the bug can be consistently reproduced, the next step in debugging is to gather data. Debugging, at its core, is a process of collecting evidence. Just like a detective investigating a crime scene, you need to use the tools at your disposal to gather as much information as possible about the system's state and behavior. These tools include debuggers, logging frameworks, unit tests, breakpoints, and any other mechanism that can give you insight into what's happening under the hood of your system. One of the most essential tools in a debugger's toolkit is the debugger itself. Modern debuggers, integrated into IDEs or used as standalone tools, allow you to pause the execution of a program, inspect variables, and step through code line by line. This gives you the ability to observe the state of your program at any given moment. It's like standing over the shoulder of the application, watching it think, and understanding exactly how it arrives at each decision. This is a critical component of the detective work.

Logging can be an invaluable tool in the investigation. While debugging tools allow you to inspect the program in real-time, logging provides a historical record of the system's behavior, especially in production environments where real-time inspection may not be feasible. By inserting logs at key points in the code, you can observe the flow of execution, capture error messages, and track variables that help pinpoint the root cause of a bug. In my experience, well-placed log statements have often been the first clue that pointed me in the right direction.

Breakpoints, which allow you to pause execution at a specific line of code, and unit tests, which help validate that smaller components of the system are working as expected, are also indispensable in debugging. They let you isolate parts of the code that seem most suspicious and inspect them in great detail, while unit tests can help you rule out issues with specific modules or functions.

An essential part of the investigative process is knowing when and how to use these tools. It's easy to become overwhelmed with the sheer volume of information that debuggers and logs can provide. A good detective knows that the key is not just gathering evidence but gathering the right evidence. Whether you're using a debugger, logging, or breakpoints, your goal is to systematically collect the data that will help you isolate the problem. The right tool, used at the right moment, can provide the crucial piece of the puzzle that allows you to move forward in your investigation.

With the tools at your disposal and the bug reproduced, the next step is to start narrowing down the potential causes. A key part of the detective work in debugging is hypothesis testing. As you gather evidence, you'll form theories about what could be going wrong. Each hypothesis needs to be tested carefully before it can be either confirmed or ruled out.

Testing hypotheses requires a systematic approach. For each theory you test, you need to observe the results and decide whether the bug is resolved or if you need to revise your theory. This is where experience comes into play as an experienced debugger can often spot patterns, make educated guesses, and focus on the areas of the code most likely to cause the issue. But even with experience, debugging is rarely a straightforward process. The ability to test multiple hypotheses, iterate, and refine your approach is an essential part of the detective work. This part of the process also requires critical thinking and a good understanding of how different parts of the system interact with each other. Bugs rarely exist in isolation. They may be caused by a single line of faulty code, but that code is often just a symptom of a deeper problem in the system's architecture or design. A good debugger knows how to trace the problem to its source, even when it's buried deep in a complex system.

A key principle in debugging is the ability to eliminate possibilities systematically. This is not about jumping to conclusions. It involves testing a series of educated guesses, each of which brings you closer to the solution by eliminating one potential cause after another. A method I've found particularly helpful is the process of binary elimination, where you progressively narrow down the scope of the investigation. For example, if you're unsure whether the issue lies with the database, the network, or the application code, you can isolate each of these components by testing them individually. First, verify that the database connection is functioning properly, then test the network layer, and finally check the application code. By isolating and eliminating each possibility, you reduce the scope of the problem until you're left with the true culprit.

One of the most common mistakes new developers make when debugging is failing to test in a structured, deliberate manner. They may jump from one hypothesis to another, making changes without clear direction, which only complicates the investigation. A detective, however, does not work this way. They follow the clues methodically, ruling out possibilities one at a time until the solution becomes apparent.

After hours of investigation, testing, and elimination, there is a moment of clarity when all the pieces fall into place. This is the moment when the bug is finally uncovered, and the root cause is discovered. It is often an anticlimax after all, the hard work is in the process, not the final solution but it's a satisfying moment, nonetheless.

The process of debugging is, without a doubt, one of the most challenging aspects of being a software engineer. But it is also one of the most rewarding. Debugging is a detective's craft, one that requires a methodical, patient, and precise approach. It's about following the evidence, testing hypotheses, and eliminating possibilities until the root cause of the problem is found.

Through determination, resilience, and a systematic approach, engineers can often overcome seemingly insurmountable issues and emerge with not just a solution, but a deeper understanding of their craft. We'll discuss why persistence is crucial in debugging, how to maintain motivation when things get tough, and how to build a mindset that keeps pushing forward, even when it feels like success is out of reach.

When you first encounter a difficult bug, it's easy to feel defeated. It's especially demoralizing when you spend hours or even days working on the issue without making any meaningful progress. You may feel like you've hit a dead end, and it's tempting to throw your hands up in frustration and move on to something else. However, it's in these moments of despair that persistence becomes your most valuable asset. A common phenomenon that many engineers experience when debugging difficult problems is a sort of "mental fatigue." Your mind starts to feel foggy, and you become emotionally drained from the sheer effort of trying to resolve the issue. It's easy to succumb to the feeling that "nothing is working" and that you should just move on to the next task. However, abandoning a bug before fully understanding it is often a mistake. The frustration and fatigue you're feeling are often signal that you're close to a breakthrough. It's at the point where you feel like giving up that persistence matters the most.

One of the most tempting pitfalls of debugging is the urge to move on when you're not getting results. It's easy to convince yourself that there's a more urgent task to tackle or that this particular bug isn't worth the time and energy. There's always a new project on the horizon, deadlines to meet, and other parts of the system that need attention. But it's precisely this attitude that leads to half-baked solutions, technical debt, and more problems down the road. The desire to move on is especially strong when dealing with bugs that feel insurmountable. You might feel like you've reached an impasse, and it's tempting to take the easier route of putting the problem aside and coming back to it later. However, every time you do that, you're simply kicking the can down the road. You're avoiding the hard work that will eventually need to be done, and you're creating a more complex future problem for yourself.

I've encountered many situations in my career where I had the option to walk away from a problem. Early on, I made the mistake of doing so, convinced that the issue would resolve itself or that someone else would fix it. But in every instance, I found that bugs left unresolved would only grow more complicated, becoming more entrenched in the system. Often, they would resurface in a way that was even harder to debug, costing me far more time and effort in the long run.

While persistence is essential for debugging, it's also important to recognize the risk of burnout. Debugging a tough issue can be draining, and without a plan for managing your energy and focus, it's easy to become mentally exhausted. The pressure to solve a bug quickly, combined with the frustration of hitting roadblocks, can easily lead to a state of burnout. I've often found that the key to avoiding burnout during long debugging sessions is knowing when to step away and recharge. Debugging is a marathon, not a sprint. If you've been struggling with a particularly difficult problem for hours or days, sometimes the best course of action is to take a break. It might seem counterintuitive after all, isn't persistence about continuing to push through? But in reality, stepping back for a moment can offer a new perspective and can help you return to the problem with a clearer mind.

Moreover, persistence doesn't mean working on the bug in isolation. It's often helpful to reach out to peers, ask for input, or pair program to get fresh insights. Collaboration and shared problem-solving can help you maintain your motivation when you feel stuck. Discussing the problem with someone else can also reveal things you might have missed. Debugging is rarely a solo activity; persistence means knowing when to lean on your team and when to take a step back to avoid mental fatigue.

There's a delicate balance between confidence and humility that plays a crucial role in persistence. On the one hand, confidence is important. As a debugger, you need to believe in your ability to solve the problem. You need to trust that your efforts will eventually lead to success. On the other hand, humility is equally essential. Debugging requires the humility to accept that you don't know everything. You must be willing to admit when you've made a mistake or missed something critical, and to be open to new possibilities and approaches.

I've seen many engineers struggle because they were either too confident or too humble. Too much confidence can lead to overconfidence, where you jump to conclusions too quickly and miss key details. On the flip side, a lack of confidence can cause you to abandon the search for a solution too soon, or to second-guess yourself constantly, which leads to indecision. The key to persistence is striking the right balance between these two qualities. You must remain confident in your ability to solve the problem, but humble enough to keep questioning your assumptions and reconsider your approach if necessary.

Persistence is not only about finding success, but also about learning from failure. Each bug, each problem you encounter, is an opportunity for growth. Even when you don't immediately solve an issue, you gain valuable experience. Every debugging session teaches you something new whether it's a new technique, a deeper understanding of your system, or a better way to approach future problems.

The ability to persist through frustration, to keep going even when things seem hopeless, is what separates great engineers from good ones. It is the engine that drives us to explore new possibilities, refine our techniques, and learn from every failure. Through persistence, we uncovered the solutions that make our software more reliable and our systems more robust.

CHAPTER THREE
From Algorithms to Architecture

As software engineers, our careers often begin with a clear and manageable task: solving small, well-defined problems. These problems typically involve writing code to implement algorithms that achieve specific goals. Whether it's a sorting algorithm to reorder a list of numbers, a search algorithm to find a specific element in a dataset, or an optimization algorithm to minimize some form of cost or loss, our early coding tasks focus on solving isolated, specific issues. The mindset required to solve these problems is one of precision, attention to detail, and logical thinking. The boundaries are defined, the inputs and outputs are clear, and success can often be measured directly by how quickly or efficiently we solve the problem.

However, as our experience grows and we are entrusted with more complex projects, we inevitably find ourselves shifting from algorithmic problem-solving to system design. This transition is a fundamental milestone in any engineer's career and involves a significant shift in the way we approach software development.

Rather than focusing on the optimization of small functions or solving one-off problems, we begin to think about how individual pieces of code and algorithms fit into the larger puzzle of the software system as a whole. The shift from writing individual lines of code to designing entire systems is not merely a matter of scale but it is a change in mindset, one that requires us to see the bigger picture and to consider how different components of a system interact, scale, and evolve over time.

The initial joy of solving small problems with algorithms gives way to the broader, more complex challenges of designing scalable, reliable, and maintainable systems. System-wide thinking introduces new layers of complexity, as decisions about architecture must take into account trade-offs, future growth, team collaboration, and the potential for change. These challenges require a different kind of thinking and one that is less about finding the perfect solution for a small problem and more about finding solutions that are sustainable and flexible enough to support an entire system's long-term needs.

In the early stages of our careers, we are often tasked with solving problems that seem self-contained. These tasks usually involve optimizing algorithms, implementing well-known data structures, and refining small sections of code. The problems are often tightly solved, with inputs and outputs that are easily defined. You might be asked to write an efficient algorithm to find the shortest path in a graph (Dijkstra's or A), implement a balanced tree (like AVL or Red-

Black tree) to handle a collection of data efficiently or optimize a function to reduce its time complexity from O(n^2) to O (n log n).

These are problems that have a well-known solution, and once implemented, they tend to be self-contained. Success is relatively straightforward to measure, did the algorithm return the correct result? Did it run within the expected time and space constraints? The focus is on correctness and efficiency, often relying on classic approaches or well-established algorithms. For engineers just starting out, these tasks provide the satisfaction of solving well-defined problems, gaining experience in coding best practices, and building a foundation in problem-solving techniques.

There is beauty in the simplicity of algorithmic thinking. When solving these problems, you are typically given a clear set of rules and a set of inputs to process. The boundaries are well-defined, and your job is to deliver a solution that fits within those boundaries. These experiences teach you the core principles of software engineering such as logic, performance, and optimization and help you develop a toolkit of algorithms and techniques that you can rely on for future tasks. However, as your experience grows, these problems begin to feel less challenging. You start to realize that most real-world software doesn't involve isolated algorithmic problems. It involves systems of interconnected pieces, each with its own set of constraints and dependencies. It's no longer enough to think of a problem in isolation, you have to think about how that problem fits into the larger context of the system you're working on.

The shift from working on isolated algorithms to thinking in terms of system-wide design is one of the most significant transformations in the career of a software engineer. It requires a fundamental change in mindset, from focusing on individual pieces of code to understanding how they fit together to form a coherent whole. The problems you solve as a software engineer expand in scope, and the complexity of the decisions you need to make grows exponentially.

In system design, the stakes are higher. Rather than optimizing a single algorithm or implementing a specific feature, you're tasked with designing an entire system, often with multiple interacting components. The goals are different as it can be performance, reliability, scalability, and maintainability are now your primary concerns, and these goals don't always align neatly with one another. This means that decisions you make at the architectural level can have profound, long-term implications. Take, for example, the transition from writing a single function that processes data to designing a distributed system that needs to handle millions of requests per minute. In the early days of your career, your task might involve writing an efficient function that processes a small dataset. You focus on the intricacies of the algorithm, perhaps worrying about optimizing a loop or finding the most efficient data structure to store the data.

However, when you transition to thinking about system-wide architecture, your mindset needs to expand to consider things like scalability (Will this function still perform well when the volume of data increases significantly? Can it scale horizontally across multiple servers?), reliability (If this component fails, what happens to the overall system? How can you ensure high availability and fault tolerance? Maintainability (As the system grows, how will this code evolve? Can you make changes without introducing significant risk or disrupting other parts of the system? It's no longer just about optimizing an algorithm; it's about ensuring that your code integrates smoothly into a larger architecture, where many components must work together to achieve a common goal. You start thinking about modularity, communication between services, and how to break down complex tasks into manageable components.

The real challenge of system design comes not from solving individual problems but from understanding how different components of the system interact with each other. Unlike isolated algorithms, where the inputs and outputs are well-defined, in system design, the interactions between components introduce a new level of complexity. Systems often consist of multiple services, APIs, databases, and user interfaces, each with its own set of requirements and constraints.

In a large system, changes in one component can have cascading effects on others. For example, a new feature that you develop may require changes to the database schema, which in turn affects the data access layer and may even require changes to the front end. As a result, thinking in terms of interactions is key to effective system design. You must account for the dependencies between components and ensure that the system as a whole remains coherent and stable even as changes are made. As you transition into architectural thinking, you begin to see how everything is interconnected. You realize that while one isolated algorithm may work perfectly fine for small inputs, once you begin to scale, the complexity of inter-component communication, data storage, error handling, and fault tolerance grows. In distributed systems, for example, you need to think about issues like data consistency (using CAP theorem), latency, partition tolerance, and how to gracefully handle failures.

The challenge here is not to design individual components in isolation, but to create an architecture where those components can work together effectively. This requires a different kind of problem-solving mindset, one that embraces the complexity of interactions, dependencies, and trade-offs between different system requirements. It's about understanding how every decision you make on one component affects the others and how you can design systems that are robust, flexible, and maintainable in the long run.

As your career progresses, you begin to shift your focus from specific algorithms to broader system design principles. This shift requires not only technical knowledge but also a set of complementary skills that enable you to design complex systems effectively. Some of these skills include:

Architectural Patterns: Learning about different architectural styles (e.g., microservices, monolithic, event-driven, layered architectures) and when to apply them based on the system's requirements.

Non-Functional Requirements: Understanding and prioritizing non-functional requirements like scalability, performance, security, and availability.

Trade-offs: Recognizing the inevitable trade-offs between different design decisions and knowing how to make the right choices based on the system's goals.

Communication and Collaboration: Since system design often involves cross-functional teams, being able to effectively communicate and collaborate with others (e.g., backend developers, product managers, operations teams) is essential.

I remember early on in my career, I would focus purely on the algorithmic efficiency of my code, tweaking loops and data structures for minimal complexity. But over time, I began to realize that no matter how efficient the code was at the micro-level, the system as a whole could still fail if the larger design was flawed. My view expanded to think not just about the best way to implement a single algorithm, but about how that algorithm fit into the overall workflow of a larger system.

The shift from working on small, isolated problems with algorithms to thinking in terms of system-wide architecture is a defining moment in a software engineer's career. It requires a shift in mindset from solving specific problems to understanding how those problems fit into a larger whole. The challenges of system design are complex and multifaceted, requiring a deep understanding of how components interact, how systems scale, and how to make decisions that ensure long-term maintainability.

This transition is not easy. It requires a broader skill set, a deeper understanding of software engineering principles, and the ability to collaborate with others. However, it is also one of the most rewarding aspects of a software engineer's career. By embracing this shift and developing your system design skills, you not only become a more effective engineer but also a more strategic thinker, capable of creating robust, scalable, and maintainable systems that can meet the challenges of the future.

The three most prominent aspects of system design that necessitate trade-offs are performance, scalability, and maintainability. These pillars often come into tension with one another, and the architect must strike a delicate balance to ensure the system is robust enough to meet both current and future demands. Understanding how to navigate these trade-offs is a key part of building systems that not only work today but are also flexible and adaptable as requirements evolve. We will explore these three aspects in detail, examining how they interrelate and how to make informed decisions that serve the long-term goals of the system.

When you begin designing a system, one of the first things you think about is performance. You want the system to be fast and responsive, particularly when dealing with large amounts of data or high user traffic. Whether it's optimizing the speed of a function or reducing latency in a network call, performance is often a key consideration, especially in the early stages of development. However, as you begin to think beyond individual components and start designing a larger system, the need to scale up becomes critical. Performance optimizations that work for small data sets or a limited number of users often break down when the system grows. Scalability concerns involve designing systems that can handle increased loads without significant degradation in performance.

The tension between performance and scalability is an inevitable part of system design. In the early stages, when the system is small, it might be acceptable to focus purely on performance. After all, you can always refactor or optimize later as the load increases. But as the system grows, that approach can cause problems. If performance optimizations are overly aggressive or focus too narrowly on small-scale performance, they may make it difficult to scale the system to meet future demands. To resolve this, you could scale the system by introducing distributed computing, which is sharding the data across multiple servers, and using parallel processing to distribute the load. But this requires an architectural shift, and it's not simply about improving the algorithm itself. You have to consider how the data is partitioned, how nodes communicate with each other, and how to maintain consistency across the system. What was once a simple in-memory solution now requiring a distributed system, and you need to be prepared for these complexities.

The key insight here is that while focusing on performance in the early stages of a project can be beneficial, it's crucial to always keep scalability in mind. Building with scalability in mind from the start can prevent significant architectural rework later. The best approach is often to design the system with scalability as a core principle, even if that means making some early compromises in performance.

Scalability is not only about handling more users or more data. It is about the long-term ability to grow without introducing unnecessary complexity. Systems that are highly scalable but poorly designed in terms of maintainability can become unwieldy over time. As new features are added and the system grows, complexity can quickly spiral out of control if the architecture doesn't support efficient changes or enhancements. When designing for scalability, one of the main trade-offs you'll face is how much complexity you are willing to introduce into the system in the name of futureproofing. It's tempting to over-engineer solutions to ensure that the system can handle 10x, 100x, or even 1000x the current load, but doing so often introduces unnecessary complexity that can make the system harder to maintain and debug.

This trade-off between scalability and maintainability can be tricky to navigate. On one hand, you want to ensure that the system can grow without breaking down, but on the other hand, you want to avoid introducing too much complexity too early, which can make maintenance and future development harder. The best practice here is to aim for scalable simplicity, which is designing the system in a way that anticipates future growth but doesn't overcomplicate things unnecessarily. A good way to approach this trade-off is by using the incremental approach. Initially, you might use simpler, less scalable solutions that get the system up and running. Once the system is functional and you have a better understanding of future needs, you can start to refactor for scalability. Engineering over-engineering early often results in a heavy, overcomplicated design that becomes difficult to modify.

The tension between performance and maintainability is perhaps one of the most subtle and insidious trade-offs you'll encounter as a software architect. In the rush to optimize a system for performance whether that's improving the runtime of a function, reducing memory usage, or decreasing latency you can easily lose sight of the long-term impact on the maintainability of the codebase.

Optimized code often sacrifices readability and simplicity for the sake of speed or efficiency. An algorithm that performs better might involve intricate optimizations that are difficult to understand or modify later. For example, an algorithm using low-level memory management techniques or highly specialized data structures may yield significant performance gains in the short term, but at the cost of making the code harder to debug, test, and maintain. In practice, performance optimizations often come at the expense of readability. Code that's harder to read and understand can lead to more bugs, more time spent on debugging, and more difficulty making changes in the future. Developers may find themselves spending more time trying to understand a highly optimized piece of code than they would have spent on a simpler, less performant solution.

To strike a balance between performance and maintainability, it's important to focus on sustainable performance. Early in the design process, it's often better to start with a simple, clear solution and optimize later when there's clear evidence that performance is a bottleneck. Optimization should be driven by actual use cases and profiling, rather than premature assumptions about performance. In other words, premature optimization is the root of all evil which is a well-known principle in software engineering. It's better to first design with clarity and simplicity and then optimize the critical paths once the system is running in production.

The core challenge of system design is managing the delicate balance between performance, scalability, and maintainability. These three pillars are interconnected and must be treated as parts of an integrated whole rather than as isolated concerns.

To navigate this balance, you should use a holistic approach to system design. Rather than optimizing for one aspect in isolation, always consider how changes to one pillar (e.g., performance) will impact the others (e.g., scalability and maintainability). Use a feedback loop in which you constantly evaluate trade-offs and iterate on the design as new challenges arise. Prototyping and testing are invaluable during this phase, as they allow you to explore different solutions and understand their implications before making a final decision. The ability to balance performance, scalability, and maintainability is what separates junior engineers from senior engineers and architects. Senior engineers understand that architecture isn't just about solving today's problems; it's about anticipating tomorrow's challenges and designing systems that can evolve, scale, and adapt over time.

Balancing performance, scalability, and maintainability is one of the most difficult yet rewarding aspects of system architecture. These trade-offs are a natural part of software design and reflect the inherent complexity of building systems that are not only performant but also sustainable and adaptable in the long term. The key is to understand how each decision you make impacts the system as a whole and to design systems that are capable of evolving over time without sacrificing critical qualities.

We will now focus on the critical skill of designing software that is flexible and adaptable. We'll explore the concept of futureproofing, the techniques for creating systems that can evolve smoothly, and the strategies that architects use to ensure that software continues to meet new requirements without requiring a complete redesign. Designing for the future requires a mindset that prioritizes changeability, resilience, and sustainability. It's about preparing for the unknown while also designing a robust foundation that allows for ongoing iteration, refactoring, and innovation.

Software development, especially in large systems, is inherently unpredictable. The requirements you start with often evolve dramatically as the project progresses. New stakeholders, market shifts, performance bottlenecks, changing user needs, and external technologies (e.g., cloud services, new programming languages) can all alter the landscape. Systems that were designed for a specific use case or a particular set of assumptions may become outdated as the business scales, new features are introduced, or new patterns of usage emerge. For example, consider the rapid changes that occur in the tech industry. In the early 2000s, a lot of software was designed to run on monolithic servers, often with tightly coupled code and databases. But as cloud computing and microservices architectures gained popularity, many of these systems had to undergo significant re-architecture to support distributed systems. A system designed in 2005 for a simple use case might no longer meet the needs of the company in 2025 due to changing traffic patterns, usage habits, and the addition of new business requirements.

This reality means that software architects must build systems that can accommodate change and avoid becoming rigid or brittle. The concept of "futureproofing" is thus central to software architecture. But what does it mean to future-proof a system, and how can architects ensure that the system remains adaptable over time?

One of the most powerful tools available to architects who want to design adaptable systems is the principle of modularity. Modularity refers to breaking a system into smaller, independent components, each with a well-defined interface. This enables each component to be developed, tested, and deployed independently, which makes it easier to modify or replace parts of the system without disrupting the entire application. The benefits of modularity are clear: it allows for incremental changes and improvements, reduces the risk of breaking existing functionality, and makes it easier to swap out components as new technologies and paradigms emerge. This approach allows software systems to evolve gradually and incrementally, with each change being low-risk and well-controlled.

Modularity also facilitates the adoption of new technologies over time. For example, if a new, more efficient data store becomes available, you can integrate it into the existing system without having to redesign the entire application. The modular architecture allows you to replace the old database with the new one without impacting the business logic or user interface components, ensuring minimal disruption.

When designing a system for the future, it's not enough to simply optimize what you know today. Architects must also anticipate future requirements that may arise as the business or technology evolves. This requires not just technical expertise, but also an understanding of the broader trends in the industry and the specific needs of the business. Anticipating change is one of the hardest aspects of system design, but it is critical for long-term success. A system built with future requirements in mind is one that is flexible. Flexibility in this context doesn't mean being able to handle every possible scenario but rather being able to handle a broad range of changes. This may involve considering how the system will handle increasing traffic or users, business growth and technological advancements.

One of the most important tools for future-proofing a system is loosely coupling services and components. By minimizing dependencies between different parts of the system, you create more flexibility in how the system evolves. For example, if the user management service is loosely coupled from the rest of the platform, you can more easily adopt a new authentication method or integrate a third-party identity provider without disrupting other services. The key is to design with interoperability in mind, making sure that the system can accommodate new components, features, or integrations with minimal friction.

Another critical aspect of designing for the future is using abstraction to decouple the system's internal workings from its external interfaces. Abstraction allows you to hide the complexity of a system's implementation, making it easier to change the internal workings of a system without affecting external users or consumers of the system. Abstraction also plays a significant role in enabling testability and extensibility. By abstracting out complex logic into smaller, well-defined modules or services, you can isolate functionality, test it more effectively, and extend the system with new features more easily. This not only aids in system evolution but also ensures that future developers can build on the system without risking breaking the core functionality.

The best systems are not designed all at once as they evolve over time. Evolutionary design is an approach that recognizes that systems will change, and thus, architecture should be continuously refined to meet new challenges. This iterative process of refactoring and improving the system helps ensure that it continues to meet new demands while maintaining a high standard of quality. The key to evolutionary design is the idea that architecture is never "finished." While it's essential to have an initial architecture in place, it should be flexible enough to accommodate changes as new features are introduced, new technologies are adopted, and unforeseen challenges arise. The initial design should not be overly rigid or exhaustive but should instead provide a solid foundation on which to build. From this foundation, developers can iteratively improve the system over time.

One critical aspect of evolutionary design is creating a feedback loop between development, deployment, and testing. By continuously testing and monitoring the system in production, you gain valuable insights into how the system behaves in real-world conditions. These insights can guide future design decisions and highlight areas of the system that need improvement. As new requirements arise, you can refactor the system to support those changes while preserving the overall integrity of the architecture.

Designing software that can evolve is not just about technical decisions but also about creating a culture of adaptability within the development team. Architects must foster an environment where continuous learning, iteration, and improvement are prioritized. This involves encouraging collaboration, knowledge sharing, and a willingness to embrace change.

A culture of adaptability also means building systems that are easy to document and onboard new developers. As teams grow and evolve, new engineers will need to quickly understand the system and contribute to its development. Well-documented systems that provide clear guidance on how the architecture works and how different components interact will make it much easier to bring new developers on board and allow them to contribute to the system's evolution.

Designing systems for the future requires a combination of foresight, flexibility, and adaptability. While it is impossible to predict exactly what changes will come, architects must design systems that can handle evolving requirements, new technologies, and unforeseen challenges. By building systems with modularity, abstraction, and flexibility at their core, software engineers can ensure that their systems are not just solutions to today's problems, but adaptable platforms capable of supporting the needs of tomorrow.

The goal of future proofing is not to design a system that can handle everything, but to design one that is resilient in the face of change, one that can evolve gracefully, scale efficiently, and integrate with new technologies as they emerge.

CHAPTER FOUR
Writing Code: Building Trust, The Human Side Of Software Engineering

In the world of software engineering, it's easy to become consumed by the intricacies of code, the elegance of algorithms, and the technical challenges that come with building complex systems. Yet, while these technical skills are vital to success, the true foundation of a project's success lies in communication and the ability to articulate ideas, share knowledge, and translate the technical world into terms that stakeholders from various backgrounds can understand. Software engineering, at its core, is as much about people as it is about code.

The primary goal of this section is to explore the significance of clear, effective communication in software development. We will examine the different forms of communication that software engineers engage in, why they matter so much, and how engineers can improve their communication skills to bridge the gap between technical experts and non-technical stakeholders. In particular, we'll look at how strong communication helps foster collaboration, align expectations, and ultimately drive the success of projects, whether they're in early stages of ideation, development, or ongoing maintenance.

Clear communication builds trust between developers and stakeholders, a crucial foundation for effective collaboration. By translating technical jargon into layman's terms, addressing stakeholder concerns with empathy, and actively listening to feedback, software engineers can not only build more user-friendly systems but also create a culture of openness, transparency, and mutual respect.

One of the key challenges in software development is the language barrier between developers and non-technical stakeholders. When engineers work on the back end of a system, they tend to use specific jargon, such as "APIs," "microservices," or "CI/CD pipelines," which is second nature to them but often baffling to non-technical stakeholders like product managers, designers, or clients. A developer's ability to distill complex technical concepts into simple, comprehensible explanations is critical to building trust and ensuring that everyone involved in the project is aligned.

Being able to explain technical decisions in clear, simple terms also ensures that stakeholders can understand trade-offs. For example, a decision to prioritize performance over scalability may make sense in the short term but could cause problems down the road as the system grows. If developers can explain this clearly e.g. "We've chosen this approach because it will allow us to meet the immediate performance goals, but it will require reworking later as the system scales", stakeholders can make more informed choices and manage their expectations accordingly.

Equally important to communication is the ability to listen actively. In software development, particularly in agile or iterative environments, the requirements and goals often evolve over time. Stakeholders, whether they're clients, product owners, or even end-users, frequently have valuable insights into the needs and priorities of the business. The role of the software engineer is not just to execute technical solutions but also to understand the underlying business goals and translate them into practical, technical solutions.

Active listening involves giving full attention to the speaker, asking, clarifying questions, and responding thoughtfully. By doing so, engineers gain a deeper understanding of the business challenges and user needs behind the project, allowing them to craft solutions that truly meet the intended objectives. This is particularly critical when working with non-technical stakeholders who may not have the same fluency in technical concepts but are experts in their domain.

Imagine a scenario where a product manager discusses the need for a new feature that will improve user engagement. The product manager might not be able to explain the precise technical requirements, but by asking the right questions and engaging in a dialogue, the engineer can uncover the true purpose of the feature. Maybe the product manager's goal is to increase user retention, but the engineer might suggest a slightly different approach such as adding personalized notifications instead of gamifying the app that could achieve the same result more efficiently. Active listening allows the engineer to align the technical work with the business objectives and ensure that the solution being developed solves the right problem. Furthermore, actively listening to user feedback and observing consistent interactions with the system can provide invaluable insights that guide future development. In a world where requirements can shift rapidly due to competitive pressures or changing market conditions, being attuned to the needs of stakeholders helps ensure that the software being developed remains relevant and effective.

While verbal communication is critical, clear, concise, written documentation plays an equally significant role in ensuring smooth communication within a software development team and between developers and stakeholders. Documentation acts as the bridge between the initial vision and its execution. It ensures that knowledge is preserved, and that stakeholders, both technical and non-technical, have a reference they can turn to when needed.

Many developers tend to neglect documentation in favor of focusing on writing code. However, well-documented systems help ensure that decisions made today are understood tomorrow. Clear documentation is essential for aligning team members and ensuring that everyone understands the architecture, design decisions, and rationale behind the code. When engineers document the reasoning behind specific design or architectural decisions, they also ensure continuity in the project. Team members who join the project later on can quickly come up to speed without needing to ask the same questions or reinvent the wheel. Documentation, in this sense, is an act of communication that preserves the collective knowledge of the team and the broader project.

One of the most powerful tools in building trust with stakeholders is transparency. Software projects, especially those that span multiple months or years, inevitably encounter roadblocks, delays, and shifting requirements. It's easy to promise the moon and deliver only a fraction of what was expected, but this can severely damage relationships and erode trust. Instead, maintaining open lines of communication through regular updates and honest assessments of progress is vital.

Providing stakeholders with regular status reports whether through sprint reviews, bi-weekly meetings, or project dashboards ensures that everyone is on the same page. Rather than letting stakeholders be blindsided by delays or misaligned expectations, engineers should proactively communicate risks and challenges as they arise. For example, if a feature is going to take longer than expected to develop or if a technical challenge is causing delays, communicating this early allows stakeholders to adjust their expectations accordingly and collaborate on solutions. They may even be able to offer additional resources or suggest alternate paths forward that the development team hadn't considered.

Transparency is also crucial when there are technical limitations or trade-offs involved. Instead of pretending that everything is perfect, engineers should feel empowered to communicate the risks and constraints they face. By discussing these openly, teams can come to a consensus about the best path forward, and stakeholders can make more informed decisions about scope, timeline, and priorities.

Software development often involves navigating ambiguity, particularly in the early stages of a project. Clients or stakeholders may have a general idea of what they want, but the details are often vague or constantly changing. The developer's ability to communicate through these uncertainties is important to preventing misunderstandings and ensuring that the system ultimately meets the business needs.

In these situations, it's important for software engineers to ask clarifying questions and make sure they fully understand the requirements. Ambiguity often leads to incorrect assumptions, and those assumptions can result in wasted time and effort. Sometimes, developers must also be proactive in defining the problem before starting development. In scenarios where the requirements aren't clear, it can be helpful for engineers to provide prototypes, mockups, or proofs of concept to facilitate discussions. These tools can help clarify the scope and reduce the risk of misunderstandings.

By seeking clarification and handling uncertainty with an open, collaborative mindset, developers can ensure that they are always working towards the right goals and that the final product aligns with the stakeholders' vision.

In software engineering, success is rarely achieved in isolation. While the allure of individual brilliance and technical prowess is often emphasized in our profession, the reality is that building robust, scalable, and sustainable software systems is almost always a team effort. Software engineering projects are complex endeavors that require diverse skill sets, perspectives, and experiences. Collaboration, therefore, is a cornerstone of software development, and understanding how to work effectively with others is one of the most important skills that engineers can develop.

Trust is the bedrock upon which successful collaboration is built. Without trust, team members may hesitate to share ideas, offer feedback, or admit mistakes. In software development, where the stakes are often high and the complexity can be overwhelming, a lack of trust can lead to miscommunication, duplicated effort, and ultimately, a failed project. On the other hand, a team with a strong foundation of trust can achieve great things, with each member contributing their expertise and feeling confident that others are doing the same.

Trust within a team doesn't happen overnight. It's built through consistent, honest communication, shared experiences, and an understanding that everyone is working toward the same goal. In a high-trust team, individuals feel comfortable being vulnerable whether that means asking for help, proposing a new idea, or admitting when they don't know something. This openness leads to better collaboration, as team members can approach challenges together rather than working in silos.

For software engineers, trust manifests in several ways. For instance, when a developer writes code, they must trust that their colleagues will review it thoughtfully and provide constructive feedback, not just criticism. Similarly, when discussing design decisions, engineers must trust that input from non-technical team members such as product managers and designers will be taken into account and considered valid. When developers trust that their teammates have the same dedication to quality and success, they are more likely to take risks, innovate, and challenge assumptions, all of which can lead to better software.

Collaboration doesn't just happen through meetings or casual conversations; it also happens through direct interaction with the codebase. Two widely used collaboration techniques in software development are pair programming and code reviews which are powerful tools that can improve the quality of the software while strengthening the team dynamic.

Pair programming involves two developers working together on the same task: one writes the code (the "driver"), while the other reviews the code and thinks through the design decisions (the "navigator"). This technique encourages efficient collaboration and knowledge sharing. While it may initially seem inefficient to have two people working on the same task, the benefits often outweigh the costs. Pair programming fosters greater code quality, as the navigator can spot mistakes or suggest better approaches in real time, leading to fewer bugs and cleaner code. Moreover, it allows developers to share expertise whether it's helping junior developers level up or providing a sounding board for new ideas. It also creates a space for discussion, where developers can align technical decisions and ensure that the code is both technically sound and aligned with the project's goals.

However, effective pair programming requires a strong sense of mutual respect and the ability to communicate effectively. The driver must be open to suggestions from the navigator, and the navigator must offer feedback in a constructive, non-judgmental manner. If either party becomes defensive or resistant to input, the collaboration will suffer, and the benefits of pair programming will be diminished.

Code reviews are another powerful collaboration technique that is central to modern software development practices. Code reviews allow developers to examine one another's work and provide feedback before changes are merged into the codebase. This practice not only improves code quality but also encourages collaboration across the team. During code reviews, developers can point out potential issues, suggest improvements, and discuss design decisions in the context of the larger system. This feedback loop fosters learning and knowledge sharing, as developers are exposed to different coding styles and approaches.

Code reviews also help ensure that the team is aligned with technical standards and best practices. Through consistent code reviews, developers can maintain a uniform coding style, reduce technical debt, and ensure that code is understandable by others. Moreover, code reviews offer an opportunity for junior developers to learn from more experienced engineers, leading to the overall improvement of the team's skills and expertise. The key to successful code reviews lies in providing constructive feedback, focusing on the code itself rather than personal criticisms and maintaining a culture of collaboration rather than one of judgment or criticism.

No matter how well a team communicates or how much trust exists among its members, conflicts are inevitable. Whether they're technical disagreements, personality clashes, or differences in opinion about project priorities, conflicts can arise at any time. However, how these conflicts are handled can make the difference between a team that thrives and one that breaks down under pressure. Effective conflict resolution requires a combination of emotional intelligence, empathy, and problem-solving skills. When a conflict arises, the first step is to acknowledge it and allow team members to express their concerns. It's important to create an environment where everyone feels safe to voice their opinions without fear of retribution or dismissal. This openness allows conflicts to be addressed early, before they escalate into more significant issues.

The role of a software engineer in conflict resolution is not only to advocate for their technical perspective but also to listen to and understand the viewpoints of others. In a collaborative environment, different team members bring different strengths to the table. In addition to resolving conflicts, it's equally important to prevent them by fostering a positive team culture. A culture that promotes psychological safety, respect, and inclusiveness encourages healthy debate, creative problem-solving, and collaboration. In such a culture, team members are not afraid to ask questions, share ideas, or challenge assumptions. They know that their contributions will be valued, and they will be given the opportunity to grow and learn.

Encouraging diversity within the team also plays a significant role in fostering a positive culture. Teams with diverse backgrounds, perspectives, and skill sets tend to approach problems more creatively, resulting in better solutions. Diverse teams are also better equipped to identify and address biases, which can lead to more inclusive and user-friendly products.

One of the most powerful ways to foster collaboration within a team is through mentorship and knowledge sharing. The practice of mentoring allows more experienced developers to pass on their expertise to junior or less experienced team members, creating a culture of continuous learning and improvement. Mentorship isn't just about teaching coding techniques; it's about imparting problem-solving strategies, helping others navigate the challenges of the profession, and fostering confidence in their abilities. Mentorship also benefits the mentors themselves, as teaching and guiding others forces them to reflect on their own practices and solidify their understanding.

Beyond formal mentorship, knowledge sharing plays a critical role in fostering collaboration. Knowledge sharing can take many forms, from informal discussions and "lunch-and-learns" to more structured documentation and presentations. The goal is to ensure that everyone has access to the information they need to contribute to the project's success. This helps prevent the creation of knowledge silos, where only a few individuals hold critical information. A team that actively shares knowledge is more resilient and adaptable to changes in personnel, technology, or project direction.

It is also important to strike a balance between individual contributions and collective team goals. Software engineers must remain focused on the overall objectives of the project and ensure that their individual work aligns with the team's goals. At the same time, they should continue to bring their unique expertise and perspectives to the table, contributing to the diversity of thought within the team. This balance requires a mindset of shared ownership. Rather than thinking of success or failure as a reflection of individual performance, successful teams view their work as a collective effort.

Team members celebrate each other's successes, share the burden of challenges, and support one another in achieving common goals. When engineers embrace the idea of shared ownership, they are more likely to collaborate openly, help others when needed, and align their efforts with the larger vision.

Software engineers wield incredible power. The systems, applications, and platforms they build shape the way society functions, interact, and communicates. In a world that is increasingly dependent on technology, the consequences of their decisions extend far beyond the lines of code they write. Whether it's a piece of software used by millions of people, or a complex backend system that supports critical infrastructure, the ethical considerations surrounding software engineering are vast and impactful. As engineers, we must confront questions not only of how to build software, but why and for whom we build it.

Ethics in software engineering is not a new concept, but it has grown in importance as technology continues to integrate deeply into every aspect of our lives. Software engineers now hold a central role in determining how technology affects privacy, accessibility, security, and even the societal impact of the tools we create.

This area can often be complex and fraught with dilemmas. Decisions made in the design, development, or deployment phases can have unintended consequences, and what may seem like an innocent choice can, in hindsight, have negative social, environmental, or economic effects. As professionals responsible for these decisions, software engineers must constantly be vigilant about how their work influences individuals, communities, and society as a whole. By embracing ethical principles and striving to make decisions based on integrity and accountability, software engineers can help ensure that technology serves the greater good.

To truly understand the ethical responsibility of a software engineer, we must first recognize the magnitude of the impact our work can have. Technology influences nearly every aspect of modern life: healthcare, education, communication, entertainment, politics, finance, and more. A single line of code might inadvertently cause a major data breach, allow an algorithm to perpetuate biases, or infringe upon a user's privacy. Alternatively, a well-designed system could empower individuals, protect critical information, or improve lives in ways previously unimaginable. It requires an awareness of the long-term consequences of technology. As engineers, we are not just building systems for today, but for the future. The technologies we create can be used for both positive and negative endings, and as such, it is critical that we apply our expertise and judgment responsibly.

This responsibility is not limited to issues of privacy and security but also encompasses broader societal considerations. We must think critically about the potential for our work to reinforce or challenge existing inequalities, exacerbate social issues, or contribute to environmental degradation. Software engineers have the power to influence trends in everything from access to information to climate change mitigation. With this power comes an obligation to consider the broader implications of our work and to act in ways that prioritize the well-being of all people, not just the interests of specific stakeholders.

One of the most critical ethical issues faced by software engineers today is user privacy. With the increasing digitization of personal data such as social media activity, purchasing habits, health records, and even biometric data, software engineers are tasked with ensuring that sensitive information is handled with the utmost care. Yet, despite the growing concerns over privacy, many software systems are built in ways that disregard user data protection in favor of profits or convenience. Consider the case of data breaches: hackers gaining access to personal information, including passwords, credit card numbers, and medical history. The impact on individuals can be devastating, leading to financial loss, identity theft, and even psychological distress. But breaches are not always the result of malicious intent; they can also occur due to poor design, inadequate security measures, or even simple negligence on the part of software developers.

The ethical responsibility here is clear as software engineers must design systems with user privacy in mind from the outset. This includes the following best practices for data encryption, implementing access controls to restrict who can view or edit sensitive information, and adopting a minimization approach, collecting only the data that is strictly necessary. However, ethical software engineering goes beyond just technical measures. Engineers must also consider user consent and transparency. It's not enough to simply secure data; users should have a clear understanding of what data is being collected, how it will be used, and what control they have over it. Building trust with users means being honest and transparent about data practices and giving them the ability to make informed choices about what they share.

Closely related to privacy is the ethical responsibility software engineers have to ensure the security of their systems. Security isn't just a technical concern but an ethical obligation. Software engineers must take reasonable steps to protect their users from security threats, such as hacking, phishing, and malware. Failing to do so doesn't just jeopardize user data; it can result in serious harm. One high-profile example of security negligence is the case of Equifax, a major credit reporting agency that suffered a massive data breach in 2017. The breach exposed the personal information of over 140 million people, including social security numbers, birth dates, and addresses. The cause of the breach was traced back to a vulnerability in the company's web application software that had been known for months before the attack. The ethical issue here wasn't just the breach itself, but the failure to prioritize security and patch vulnerabilities in a timely manner. The engineers involved in this case were criticized for not following the best practices in security hygiene, including timely software updates, vulnerability scanning, and patch management.

Professionals must view security as an ethical duty, not an afterthought. This means ensuring that their code is built with security in mind, conducting regular security audits, and keeping up with the latest security standards. Moreover, engineers should embrace a security-first mindset, where security is considered at every stage of the development process, from design to deployment. This can include threat modeling, penetration testing, and building systems that are resilient to attacks. When engineers fail to protect user data and systems from harm, they not only failing to meet technical standards, but they are breaching the trust of their users.

As technology becomes more powerful, we find ourselves relying on algorithms to make critical decisions, everything from loan approvals to hiring decisions to the content we see on social media platforms. Yet, algorithms are only as good as the data fed into them, and data can be biased. This raises significant ethical issues for software engineers.

Consider the case of biased hiring algorithms that are used by companies to screen job applicants. If the data used to train these algorithms is biased, say, it reflects historical gender or racial imbalances then the algorithm may systematically favor certain candidates over others. Similarly, facial recognition technology has been found to have higher error rates for people of color and women, raising concerns about discrimination and the potential for misuse by governments or other entities. Software engineers must be keenly aware of these issues when developing AI systems and algorithms, ensuring that they are fair, transparent, and accountable.

The ethical responsibility here is twofold: first, to ensure that algorithms do not perpetuate existing biases or inequalities, and second, to be transparent about how algorithms function. Engineers should take steps to identify and mitigate biases in their data sets, engage in continuous monitoring of their systems for fairness, and ensure that algorithms are explainable, so their decisions can be understood and audited. Ultimately, software engineers must recognize that technology should empower, not oppress. By building systems that are inclusive, transparent, and fair, engineers can help prevent the entrenchment of harmful social patterns and contribute to the creation of technology that benefits all users, regardless of their race, gender, or background.

Accountability and owning our decisions is another vital aspect of the concept of ethical software engineering. Engineers must be prepared to take responsibility for their work, especially when things go wrong. In a world where software bugs, crashes, and security vulnerabilities are inevitable, the ethical obligation is to ensure that mistakes are acknowledged and corrected promptly.

They must be accountable for the long-term sustainability of their systems, ensuring that they are maintained properly, and that technical debt does not undermine their usability or security over time. Accountability also extends to being transparent about the limitations of the systems we build. When software engineers build systems, they must be honest with stakeholders about what the system can and cannot do. Misleading users or stakeholders about the capabilities of a system whether intentionally or out of ignorance violates ethical standards and damages trust.

In an era where technology is ubiquitous, software engineers cannot afford to ignore the ethical implications of their work. By embracing the principles of integrity, accountability, and transparency, and by taking proactive steps to minimize harm and maximize positive impact, software engineers can help shape a future where technology serves the greater good. After all, at the heart of ethical software engineering is the desire to create technology that empowers people, fosters trust, and contributes to a more just and equitable world.

CHAPTER FIVE

The Power of Failure: Learning to Fail Fast and Fail Forward

Failure is often viewed as a setback, a negative experience that signals a lack of competence, foresight, or ability. In software engineering, it's easy to succumb to this mindset, especially when facing frustrating bugs, missed deadlines, or disappointing product launches. However, the true power of failure lies not in its immediate discomfort, but in how we respond to it. The key to transforming failure from a roadblock into a steppingstone for success is adopting a growth mindset.

A growth mindset, as popularized by psychologist Carol Dweck, is the belief that abilities and intelligence can be developed with effort, learning, and persistence. This mindset contrasts sharply with a fixed mindset, which holds that talent and intelligence are static and unchangeable. In the world of software engineering, where challenges are constant, the difference between these two mindsets can have a profound impact on an engineer's ability to learn from failure, innovate, and ultimately succeed.

This mindset is about seeing challenges as opportunities rather than threats. For software engineers, failure is not the end of the road; it's merely a signpost that indicates there is something valuable to learn. Every bug, crash, or deployment issue is an opportunity to gain a deeper understanding of the system being built, refine a technical skill, or think creatively about alternative solutions. In traditional education or many work environments, failure is often treated as something to be avoided at all costs. Students who fail a test are seen as lacking in knowledge, and engineers who miss a deadline are sometimes labeled as inefficient or unproductive. However, in the context of software development, failure is an essential part of the iteration and problem-solving process. As we build complex systems, failure is inevitable. The challenge is not to avoid failure but to learn how to fail gracefully and use that experience to grow stronger.

To develop a growth mindset in software engineering, engineers must first reframe their understanding of failure. Rather than seeing failure as a personal flaw, it should be viewed as a necessary step toward improvement. For example, the act of failing fast, which is identifying and addressing issues early in the development process helps prevent larger issues from compounding later. In this sense, failure is not a sign of weakness but an indication that the system or approach needs refinement.

A growth mindset encourages engineers to persist in the face of difficulty and experiment with new solutions, knowing that mistakes along the way are part of the process. In fact, some of the most successful engineers and innovators in history, people like Thomas Edison, Steve Jobs, and Elon Musk have embraced failure as an essential ingredient in their creative processes. Rather than fearing failure, they use it as a springboard to iterate, pivot, and improve.

While a growth mindset is essential for turning failure into a learning opportunity, it's important to acknowledge that failure, especially in high-pressure environments like software engineering, can be emotionally taxing. When a project you've invested time and energy into doesn't work as expected, it's easy to feel defeated, frustrated, or even embarrassed. These emotions can cloud judgment, lead to burnout, or cause engineers to abandon projects prematurely. For engineers to truly embrace failure as a steppingstone, it's essential to build emotional resilience. Resilience is the ability to bounce back from setbacks, learn from adversity, and continue moving forward. Resilient engineers don't allow failure to define their worth or potential. Instead, they use it as a learning tool that sharpens their skills and makes them more effective problem solvers.

Building emotional resilience in the face of failure requires a few key practices:

Self-compassion: It's important to be kind to yourself when things don't go as planned. Mistakes and setbacks are inevitable in software engineering, and beating yourself up over them can only hinder your progress. Instead, practice self-compassion by recognizing that failure is a normal part of growth, and treat yourself with the same understanding and patience you would offer a colleague or friend in a similar situation.

Perspective: Failure often feels like the end of the road, but it's important to step back and gain perspective. Many of the world's most successful engineers and entrepreneurs experienced numerous failures before achieving their breakthroughs. For example, Elon Musk's early ventures, such as Zip2 and X.com, faced significant challenges before he found success with companies like Tesla and SpaceX. By viewing failure as a temporary setback rather than a permanent defeat, engineers can maintain their motivation and focus on the next opportunity.

Seeking support: Failure is less isolating when it's shared with others. When engineers face setbacks, it can be beneficial to reach out to colleagues, mentors, or peers for advice and encouragement. This collaborative approach fosters a culture of openness, where failure is discussed openly and used as a learning opportunity rather than something to hide or fear. Building a support network that provides constructive feedback, empathy, and guidance can help engineers move past failure more quickly and confidently.

Reflection and learning: Emotional resilience is strengthened through the ability to reflect on failure. After encountering a setback, it's crucial to analyze what went wrong, identify what could have been done differently, and make a concrete plan for improvement. Engineers who take the time to conduct post-mortems or retrospectives after each failure are more likely to turn those experiences into actionable insights that can improve their future work.

A pivotal principle that software engineers can adopt to embrace failure is the idea of "failing fast." The concept of failing fast means identifying when a solution is not working early in the process, rather than allowing issues to compound and become harder to fix later. This approach encourages engineers to experiment, iterate, and test frequently, accepting that failure will happen but ensuring it occurs early when the cost of failure is low.

Failing fast is particularly valuable in agile software development methodologies, which emphasize rapid iterations and continuous improvement. In these environments, engineers are encouraged to build small, manageable pieces of software and deploy them quickly, testing bugs and issues along the way. This allows for rapid feedback and enables the team to identify and address problems before they grow into more significant challenges. It is not just about technical issues, but also about recognizing when a project or direction is not aligned with the overall goals. For instance, if the team realizes halfway through development that a proposed feature will not meet the user needs or business objectives, they can pivot early, saving valuable time and resources. In the long run, this approach leads to better products and more efficient development cycles, as the team avoids wasting time on ideas that aren't working.

A growth mindset encourages engineers to view failure as part of an ongoing process of learning and refinement. To do this effectively, it's crucial to have continuous feedback loops in place. Feedback is essential for understanding where mistakes were made and how to improve upon them. Without feedback, failure can lead to stagnation rather than growth.

In the context of software engineering, feedback can come from various sources: code reviews, user testing, automated testing tools, and even self-reflection. Regular feedback helps engineers make small, iterative improvements that compound over time, ultimately leading to better solutions. Feedback also allows engineers to learn not just from their successes but from their failures. It enables them to iterate on their work, tweak approaches, and make better decisions moving forward.

When software engineers embrace failure as a necessary part of the development process, they position themselves to take risks, experiment with new ideas, and innovate in ways that wouldn't be possible if they were focused solely on avoiding failure. Failure is an essential part of learning especially in the ever-evolving field of software engineering and when engineers adopt the mindset that failure is feedback, they can build systems that are not only functional but resilient, efficient, and amazing.

Failure, far from being an obstacle, is often the driving force behind the most significant breakthroughs and innovations in software engineering. The idea that failure can fuel creativity and drive innovation may seem counterintuitive, especially in a field where precision and efficiency are paramount. However, some of the greatest advances in technology have arisen from the ashes of failure, where engineers, rather than giving up or shying away from their mistakes, have used them as opportunities to rethink their approaches, challenge assumptions, and develop entirely new ways of solving problems. We will look at how setbacks lead to deeper insights, how embracing failure encourages creative problem solving, and how many of the most revolutionary products and ideas in technology have emerged not in spite of failure, but because of it.

Failure as a Catalyst for Rethinking Assumptions: One of the most powerful ways failure drives innovations is by forcing engineers to question their assumptions. When an approach fails, it highlights the limitations or gaps in the original thinking, creating a natural moment of reflection and reevaluation. This is especially critical in software development, where assumptions about user behavior, performance, or the underlying technology can often go unchallenged. Consider, for instance, the story of Google Maps. In the early days of its development, Google's map-building team faced numerous technical and conceptual setbacks. One of the major challenges was how to effectively display maps at different zoom levels without compromising speed or clarity. Initially, the team was stuck on trying to render large, static images of maps, but this approach didn't work well for the dynamic zooming and smooth user interactions they wanted. It was a failure in their approach that pushed the engineers to reconsider the entire system architecture. This failure led to the development of vector-based maps, where the data for the map was rendered dynamically in real-time based on the zoom level. This breakthrough transformed Google Maps from a static, clunky service into a sleek, interactive tool that became ubiquitous worldwide.

In this case, failure was not just a setback, it was a prompt to rethink how the technology could function. The team didn't give up after their initial failure; they adapted, shifted their perspective, and ultimately created an innovation that revolutionized the mapping industry. Failure often leads to moments where engineers are forced to challenge their core assumptions, leading to insights that pave the way for entirely new approaches and paradigms.

Failure Fosters Experimentation and Risk-Taking: Failure encourages experimentation which is an essential ingredient in innovation. In software engineering, experimentation is necessary for testing ideas, iterating designs, and exploring different solutions to a problem. When engineers are comfortable with failure, they are more likely to take risks, explore unconventional approaches, and push the boundaries of what's possible. For instance, consider the development of Facebook's news feed. When Mark Zuckerberg and his team first launched the feature, it was met with significant backlash from users, who felt uncomfortable with the idea of their activities and updates being displayed so prominently. The feature was initially considered a failure, and it was even discussed as a potential rollback. However, instead of abandoning the feature entirely, the team iterated on it, using the initial failure as feedback to refine the user experience. They introduced more controls, offered personalized filters, and improved the algorithm to show more relevant content to users. What began as a failure in the eyes of many became one of the defining features of the Facebook experience.

In this case, the team's willingness to experiment and embrace failure allowed them to refine their approach and create a product that would go on to have a profound impact on how people interact with social media. If the team had been hesitant to move forward after the initial failure, they would have missed an opportunity to innovate. The ability to fail quickly, learn from the experience, and then pivot based on that learning is a hallmark of innovative thinking in software engineering.

Turning Failure into Opportunity: Learning and Iterating: In software engineering, failure is often not final; it's the beginning of a new cycle of learning and iteration. The key is in how engineers respond to failure. Instead of allowing failure to be a roadblock, the most successful engineers use it as a springboard to improve their designs, refine their processes, and try new approaches. The concept of "fail fast" is central to this mindset, as it encourages engineers to quickly identify problems and use the failure as an opportunity to make adjustments before the issue becomes too costly. For example, consider the development of early video games. Games like Minecraft and Angry Birds both started from relatively humble beginnings, with initial prototypes that didn't quite work or gain traction in the market. But the developers of these games didn't view these failures as the end of the line. Instead, they treated them as learning opportunities, iterating on the core ideas, refining gameplay mechanics, and continually testing new features. Through this iterative process, both games evolved from failures into massive successes. This approach to learning from failure is integral not only to individual engineers but also to entire teams. When teams view failure as part of the iterative process, they are more likely to take risks, experiment, and work collaboratively to solve problems. They understand that failure is not a sign of incompetence but an indicator of an evolving process that is moving towards a better solution.

Failure Sparks Creative Problem-Solving; It forces software engineers to engage in creative problem-solving. When a solution doesn't work, engineers are tasked with finding new ways to approach the problem. In fact, some of the most groundbreaking innovations come not from the first attempt but from the trial-and-error process that follows. Each failure becomes an opportunity to think outside the box, challenge existing constraints, and discover more elegant or effective solutions. For example, the development of cloud computing was initially hampered by numerous challenges and failures related to scalability, reliability, and cost. The early models of cloud infrastructure didn't meet the demands of enterprise-scale applications, and many companies faced significant setbacks in their attempts to build large-scale cloud systems. However, these early failures prompted companies like Amazon to rethink the way they approached cloud architecture. Amazon's experience with its own infrastructure failures led to the development of Amazon Web Services (AWS), which redefined the cloud computing industry. By leveraging the lessons learned from earlier failures, AWS became a leader in cloud infrastructure, providing scalable, cost-effective, and reliable services to businesses worldwide. In this case, failure was the catalyst for rethinking an entire industry. Engineers at Amazon didn't view the early setbacks as obstacles; instead, they used them as opportunities to rethink how cloud services could be delivered in a way that was more efficient and scalable. The failure to meet the original expectations led directly to a new approach which is one that would go on to disrupt the technology landscape.

Failure in Software Engineering: A Long-Term Advantage: Failure is an inevitable part of the process. However, it is through the systematic analysis of failures that engineers gain the insights and knowledge that lead to breakthrough innovations. A culture that encourages embracing failure rather than avoiding it promotes continuous improvement, drives creative solutions, and ensures that engineers are always learning and evolving. It leads to resilience, which is the ability to bounce back from setbacks and use those experiences to improve. It promotes adaptability, ensuring that engineers are always refining their skills, testing new ideas, and learning from their mistakes. And, most importantly, failure fosters an environment where innovation can thrive. By failing forward and viewing failure as an integral part of the problem-solving process, software engineers have the freedom to take risks, challenge assumptions, and ultimately create technologies that push the boundaries of what's possible.

In the end, failure is not something to be feared but embraced. It's through our failures that we learn the most, and it's those lessons that enable us to build better, more resilient systems. The most innovative software solutions don't arise from the avoidance of failure but from the willingness to fail, learn, and grow.

CHAPTER SIX
Crafting Software with Purpose and Elegance

Clean code is code that is simple, readable, and understandable. It is code that communicates its intent clearly and can be modified or extended with minimal effort. Whether you're working alone on a project or as part of a team, clean code improves the development process, reduces the risk of bugs, and makes long-term maintenance easier. The art of writing clean code is rooted in the principle that software should be a reflection of human understanding not just for the machine that runs it, but for the humans who read, modify, and build upon it. While there are numerous techniques and guidelines to follow when writing clean code, the key ideas remain simple: writing code that is easy to read, easy to change, and easy to test.

What does it mean to write "clean" code? Clean code is often described as code that is easy to read, simple to understand, and intuitive to modify. It's code that communicates its purpose effectively and has a clear structure. While clean code can vary in style and form depending on the language and the context, the core values remain the same.

The main principles are readability, simplicity, consistency, modularity and self-documenting. In readability, it is easy for someone else to read and understand what the code is doing, even if they weren't the original author. Simplicity means it doesn't overcomplicate things; it avoids clever tricks or overly intricate solutions. Consistency means the code follows consistent patterns and naming conventions. Modularity is when code is divided into small, manageable pieces, each with a clear responsibility while self-documenting refers to good names and structure which can often replace the need for excessive comments.

Clean code serves a dual purpose: it benefits the immediate team by providing clarity and reducing the chance of introducing bugs, but it also supports future developers who will inevitably work with the code long after the original author has moved on. One of the cornerstones of clean code is simplicity. Simple code is not only easier to understand, but it is also more maintainable. Simple code requires fewer resources to develop, test, and debug. The key to simplicity is avoiding unnecessary complexity, complexity introduced by convoluted logic, overly abstracted solutions, or unnecessary dependencies.

There are several ways in which simplicity manifests in code such as reducing unnecessary abstraction. While abstraction is an important tool in software design, overuse of it can make code harder to follow. The right level of abstraction is essential. Too many layers of abstraction obscure the real problem and make debugging and maintaining the code difficult.

A second method is eliminating duplication. Repeated code blocks, or "duplicate code," are a common source of errors and a maintenance nightmare. When you encounter a piece of code that appears multiple times in different places, it should be refactored into a function or method. This is a practice often referred to as DRY (Don't Repeat Yourself). By eliminating duplication, you not only make the code more maintainable but also reduce the chances of bugs when modifications are made. Limiting the scope of functions and methods is also essential. Functions should do one thing and do it well. A function that handles multiple tasks is harder to understand, harder to test, and more prone to errors. Instead, break complex functions down into smaller, more focused methods, each of which has a single responsibility.

Avoiding cleverness is another method. It's tempting to use obscure or clever programming tricks to condense code into fewer lines, but this often sacrifices clarity. For instance, using complex one-liners or relying on language-specific features that aren't widely understood can create confusion for others working on the codebase. Writing clear, direct code, even if it takes more lines, is always preferable to writing code that's hard to decipher. The clarity of your code is just as important as its simplicity. The goal is for someone reading your code (including your future self) to understand what the code is doing, why it is doing it, and how it achieves its goals with minimal effort. Code should be self-explanatory, with descriptive names and logical flow that can be easily followed.

One of the most important aspects of writing clean code is using meaningful names for variables, functions, classes, and other elements. Proper naming is often the first step in making code readable and self-documenting. In fact, a significant portion of the time spent reading code involves deciphering what each part of the code represents. If you have to continually guess the purpose of variables or functions based on vague or cryptic names, the code quickly becomes frustrating to work with. There are several best practices when it comes to naming such as descriptive names, consistency, avoiding abbreviations and using verbs for functions.

Well-named variables, functions, and classes improve the clarity of the code and reduce the need for excessive comments. If someone reads your code and immediately understands what it's doing without having to ask, you've succeeded in writing clean code.

Code structure refers to how the individual pieces of a program are organized and how they interact. A good structure makes it easier to locate specific parts of the code, follow the flow of the program, and isolate problems when they occur. Poor structure, on the other hand, leads to disorganized, hard-to-maintain code.

Some of the key principles of good code structure include Modularity. Code should be divided into small, manageable units that each have a clear, distinct responsibility. This makes it easier to test, understand, and modify specific parts of the system. Classes, functions, and methods should all serve a single purpose, and the more self-contained a piece of code is, the easier it is to modify or replace without affecting the rest of the system. Separation of concerns is another principle. This is a key design principle that dictates that different parts of a program should be responsible for different concerns. For example, business logic, user interface code, and data access code should be separated into different layers. This makes it easier to maintain and modify individual aspects of the application without affecting other parts.

Clear boundaries are boundaries between different components and should be well-defined. Code that doesn't have clear boundaries becomes tightly coupled, making it harder to test or reuse. A well-structured system is one in which components can be easily swapped or modified without breaking the entire application. While not as critical as naming, consistent formatting such as indentation, spacing, and line breaks also plays a crucial role in making code readable. Well-formatted code is easier to follow, debug, and modify. Adopting a consistent style guide for your team or organization helps ensure that everyone is on the same page.

Recognizing and refactoring problematic code is another aspect. In the world of software development, a code smell is a term used to describe any characteristic of the code that may indicate a deeper problem. These are often symptoms of poorly written code that may not cause immediate issues but will make the software harder to maintain, extend, or debug in the future. Some common code smells include duplicate codes which are repeated code that could be refactored into a shared function or class. Long functions or methods which are functions that try to do too much. They should be split into smaller, focused functions. Large classes are classes that are responsible for too many things and should be refactored into smaller, more focused classes.

The key to dealing with code smells is refactoring which is the practice of restructuring existing code without changing its functionality. By continuously refactoring and addressing these smells, developers can keep the codebase clean, efficient, and maintainable.

Writing code is not just about solving today's problem. It's about ensuring that the software you build today remains useful, understandable, and adaptable in the future. As software engineers, one of the most critical aspects of our craft is ensuring that the code we write is maintainable. Without a focus on maintainability, even the most elegant piece of software can quickly become a burden to manage, evolve, and scale. In this section, we'll explore the importance of writing maintainable code, the strategies for ensuring long-term code health, and how to balance short-term requirements with long-term sustainability.

Maintainability in software engineering refers to how easily a codebase can be modified, extended, and debugged over time. It's the quality of a software system that makes it adaptable to changes in business requirements, user needs, technology, or even the team working on it. Writing maintainable code is not simply a matter of writing code that works today; it's about writing code that can evolve, be improved upon, and be sustained with minimal friction in the future.

In software development, one of the most common misconceptions is that the value of a piece of code is only in its initial creation. The reality is that the long-term costs of maintaining that code far outweigh the cost of building it. Maintenance refers not only to fixing bugs but also to improving features, refactoring to optimize performance, and adapting to changes in the system's environment. In fact, according to some studies, maintenance costs can make up 60% to 80% of the total cost of a software project over its lifecycle. A software system is never static. It will continuously evolve as new features are added, existing features are modified, and bugs are fixed. Unmaintainable code, on the other hand, can become a liability. It's code that is difficult to understand, cumbersome to modify, and prone to introducing new issues with every change. This can lead to an accumulation of technical debt, which eventually slows down the development process, creates bottlenecks, and causes frustration among developers.

The goal, then, is to design code with maintenance in mind. By doing so, you ensure that the software remains flexible and scalable, enabling it to adapt to changing business needs and technological trends. Let's explore several key strategies that contribute to writing maintainable code.

One of the core principles of maintainability is the idea of changeability which is the ease with which code can be modified without breaking other parts of the system. The software you write today will likely need to evolve tomorrow. Whether it's adding new features, refactoring old ones, or adjusting to new business requirements, being able to change code safely and efficiently is key to maintaining a system over the long term.

Refactoring is the process of restructuring existing code without changing its external behavior, is one of the most powerful tools in maintaining a clean, adaptable codebase. Refactoring helps address technical debt, improve code quality, and enhance maintainability. By regularly refactoring the code, developers ensure that it stays drivable, that is, in a state where modifications can be made with confidence and without fear of introducing bugs.

Some common refactoring techniques include extracting methods. Long functions that try to accomplish multiple tasks can be refactored by breaking them down into smaller, more focused methods. This improves readability and makes the code easier to test. Sometimes, the original names chosen for variables or functions are unclear or misleading. Renaming them to more descriptive terms can significantly improve the clarity of the code. Complex conditional statements (e.g., `if/else` chains) can often be replaced with polymorphic behavior using inheritance or interfaces, making the code more extensible and easier to maintain. Duplicate logic scattered throughout the codebase should be reused into reusable functions or methods. This reduces the likelihood of introducing bugs when modifying one instance of duplicated code but forgetting to modify others.

Refactoring, when done regularly, helps ensure that the process evolves in a healthy, sustainable way. It prevents the accumulation of code rot, where the system becomes brittle and increasingly difficult to maintain over time due to the buildup of technical debt. However, refactoring should be approached with caution, changes must be made incrementally, with proper testing to ensure that no unintended side effects are introduced.

One of the most challenging aspects of writing maintainable code is balancing short-term requirements with long-term sustainability. It's tempting to prioritize quick solutions especially when deadlines loom or the pressure to ship features is high. However, cutting corners in the short term can create technical debt that compounds over time, making future changes increasingly difficult and costly.

In the world of software engineering, the pursuit of clean, maintainable, and readable code often runs into the age-old dilemma: how do we balance performance and elegance? On one hand, developers want their systems to run efficiently, process large volumes of data, and meet the ever-growing demands of end users. On the other hand, the core principles of clean code, simplicity, readability, and maintainability advocate for clear, concise, and understandable solutions. So, how can we reconcile these seemingly conflicting priorities? How do we ensure that the code is optimized for performance without sacrificing its elegance and long-term maintainability?

At its core, performance optimization in software engineering refers to improving the speed, efficiency, and resource utilization of a system. Whether it's making a function run faster, reducing memory consumption, or optimizing database queries, performance optimizations are crucial to ensure that applications can handle growing user bases, increasing data volumes, and more complex operations. However, when it comes to writing clean and elegant code, performance improvements sometimes come at the cost of simplicity and readability. For example, in the quest for performance, developers might introduce complex algorithms or data structures that, while faster in execution, are more difficult to understand or maintain. While performance is important, it is equally critical to consider the trade-off between optimization and code clarity. After all, software development is a long-term investment. The code that's optimized for performance today but becomes overly complicated or brittle may lead to increased maintenance costs in the future.

One of the cardinal rules in software engineering is to avoid premature optimization. This principle, popularized by Donald Knuth, suggests that developers should not optimize code until it's clear that performance improvements are necessary. The reason for this is simple: premature optimization can lead to unnecessary complexity and code bloat, as developers make changes to "improve" performance without understanding the true performance bottleneck of the system.

There are several reasons why premature optimization is often detrimental. Performance optimizations often require more complex algorithms or data structures. These solutions may be harder to understand, maintain, and debug. If the optimization isn't truly needed, the added complexity is simply a burden. Many times, what developers think is a performance issue is actually a symptom of a larger architectural problem. Without understanding where the actual performance bottleneck lies, optimizing the wrong part of the system may have little to no impact or even make things worse. Optimization efforts can consume a disproportionate amount of time and resources, delaying the release of features or bug fixes. In agile development, for example, where rapid iteration and delivery are key, optimizing prematurely can slow down the overall progress of the project.

Instead of optimizing code early on, it's better to focus on writing clear, readable, and maintainable code first. Once the code is working and the functionality is stable, performance profiling tools can be used to identify the true performance bottlenecks. After identifying the areas of the code that need optimization, developers can apply targeted optimizations that solve specific problems without introducing unnecessary complexity.

When performance optimization is necessary, the goal is to enhance the system's performance without sacrificing readability or maintainability. This is where the balance between performance and elegance becomes essential. Let's explore some strategies that can help achieve this balance.

Before making any performance improvements, it's critical to profile the application. Profiling tools allow developers to understand where the code is spending the most time or using the most resources. Rather than guessing which parts of the code need optimization, profiling provides data-driven insights into the actual performance bottlenecks. A critical factor in optimizing performance while maintaining clean code is choosing the right data structures for the job. Different algorithms and data structures have different time and space complexities. For example, using a hash table for fast lookups, or a binary search tree for efficient searching and insertion, can make a huge difference in performance.

However, selecting the optimal data structure is a balance of simple data structures and advanced structures. When choosing data structures, consider the trade-offs such as Will the performance gain from using a more complex structure justify the extra development time and the increased difficulty in maintaining the code? How well will the chosen structure fit with the rest of the system architecture? In many cases, simplicity should still be prioritized, but it's important to consider the larger performance picture, especially when dealing with critical areas like sorting, searching, or handling large datasets.

As with maintainability, performance optimizations often require refactoring. Refactoring can improve both the efficiency and the clarity of the code. In some cases, refactoring involves simplifying existing code or restructuring it to leverage more efficient algorithms or data structures. Optimizing memory usage is another critical aspect of performance, especially for applications running on devices with limited resources. Memory optimizations can reduce the likelihood of memory leaks and performance degradation due to excessive resource consumption. Some strategies include instead of creating and destroying objects repeatedly, using a pool of reusable objects to minimize memory allocation and garbage collection overhead. Tools like Valgrind or gperftools can help identify memory leaks and inefficient memory usage patterns. These tools allow developers to track memory allocation and deallocation to ensure that the system uses memory efficiently.

Again, there is a balance to be struck: while memory optimizations can improve performance, excessive memory management and optimizations can make the code harder to maintain and debug.

While the desire to improve performance is important, developers should also be wary of over-optimization. Over-optimization occurs when developers spend excessive time and resources improving performance in areas that do not provide significant gains or that compromise the elegance and maintainability of the code.

The dangers of over-optimization include increased complexity. Optimized code can become overly complicated, with intricate logic and convoluted algorithms that are difficult to understand and maintain. Optimizing areas of the code that are not performance bottlenecks can waste valuable time and effort, especially in the early stages of development. The benefits of optimization often decrease as more effort is invested. After a certain point, further optimizations may yield very little performance improvement for a lot of added complexity. The key to avoiding over-optimization is to focus on high-impact areas identified through profiling and testing. Optimize where it truly matters and ensure that each optimization makes a tangible, measurable difference in performance.

The balance between performance and elegance is one of the most challenging aspects of software development. While performance is crucial in ensuring that software is fast, responsive, and efficient, it should not come at the cost of code clarity, maintainability, and readability. By profiling the system to identify bottlenecks, selecting the right data structures, refactoring for efficiency, and leveraging concurrency, developers can optimize their code without sacrificing its elegance. Ultimately, the key is to avoid premature optimization and to focus on writing clear, maintainable code first, before applying targeted optimizations. In doing so, you ensure that your code remains both performant and elegant, allowing for long-term sustainability and ease of modification as your system evolves.

CHAPTER SEVEN
The Importance of Documentation and Knowledge Sharing

Documentation often takes a back seat to the thrill of coding and solving technical puzzles. However, as projects grow in scale and complexity, the importance of clear, concise, and well-structured documentation becomes undeniable. Great documentation serves as the backbone of any successful project, enabling teams to collaborate effectively, onboard new members efficiently, and maintain systems long after the original contributors have moved on. It is the unsung hero of long-term project success and a vital skill for engineers who aspire to leave a meaningful legacy.

Basically, documentation bridges the gap between humans and code. While code may be self-explanatory to its author in the moment, it often becomes opaque to others or even to the original author after enough time has passed. Documentation exists to provide context, explain intent, and illuminate the intricate logic that underpins software systems. Its purpose spans several domains such as onboarding new team members, facilitating collaboration, supporting maintenance and promoting accountability and transparency.

New developers can lose days or weeks trying to decipher undocumented systems. A well-documented codebase provides them with a roadmap, enabling quicker contributions and reducing the burden on senior team members for guidance. Teams thrive on shared understanding. Documentation serves as a single source of truth, ensuring all contributors are aligned on the system's architecture, design decisions, and expected outcomes. As projects evolve, maintaining legacy code becomes inevitable. Proper documentation equips developers to debug, refactor, and expand the system without unintended side effects. By recording design decisions, trade-offs, and known limitations, documentation holds engineers accountable and ensures informed decision-making for future changes.

Not all documentation is created equal. Poorly written or outdated documentation can be as frustrating as its absence. To maximize its utility, documentation must adhere to several key principles such as clarity, conciseness, structure, relevance, and accessibility. Documentation should be easy to read and understand, even for individuals unfamiliar with the system. Avoid overly technical jargon unless it is explained. Use simple, direct language to communicate complex ideas. Brevity is essential. Bloated documentation deters readers and obscures critical information. Aim to include only what is necessary to understand the system or process.

A logical organization is crucial. Use headings, subheadings, bullet points, and numbered lists to create a clear hierarchy of information. This allows readers to navigate the document efficiently and find what they need without unnecessary frustration. It should always reflect the current state of the system. Outdated or inaccurate information is worse than none because it misleads and wastes time. Establish processes to keep documentation updated alongside code changes. Ensure documentation is easy to locate and accessible to all stakeholders. This might involve hosting it on a centralized platform, ensuring it is properly indexed, or linking it directly within the codebase.

Documentation in software engineering comes in many forms, each serving a distinct purpose. While not every project requires exhaustive coverage in all areas, understanding these types helps teams prioritize their efforts. First is a code comment. These are inline comments which explain specific sections of code. While code comments are not a substitute for documentation, they provide immediate context for tricky implementations or non-obvious decisions. The second is API documentation. APIs are often the primary interface between systems or teams. Comprehensive API documentation ensures that consumers understand how to integrate with and use the system effectively. The architecture and design docs are the third. These documents capture high-level overviews of the system, including its structure, data flow, and major design decisions. They are invaluable for onboarding and long-term maintenance.

User guides and manuals are the fourth type. For end-users or clients, user guides provide step-by-step instructions and clarify how to interact with the system. They are typically less technical and more focused on functionality.For systems in production, runbooks contain procedures for handling common operational tasks or incidents, such as deployments, monitoring, and troubleshooting. Finally, we have project documentation. This includes meeting notes, decision logs, and retrospectives, capturing the context behind project milestones and challenges.

Despite its importance, documentation is often neglected or done poorly. Some common pitfalls include. Including every minor detail can overwhelm readers and make key information harder to find. Documentation should focus on the "why" and "how" rather than regurgitating code. Without maintenance, documentation becomes stale and misleading. Integrating documentation updates into the development process mitigates this risk. Writers often assume readers share their level of understanding. However, documentation must cater to a broad audience, including beginners and non-technical stakeholders. Lack of visual aids can also prove to be a challenge. Complex concepts are easier to grasp with diagrams, flowcharts, and screenshots. Text alone is not always sufficient for clarity. When no one is responsible for maintaining documentation, it quickly becomes neglected. Assigning ownership ensures accountability and continuous improvement.

Creating effective documentation requires deliberate effort and strategy. The following best practices can elevate the quality and impact of your documentation: Start Early. Documentation should begin alongside the development process. This ensures that critical insights and decisions are captured while they are still fresh. Documentation is a team effort. Involving multiple perspectives ensures comprehensive coverage and prevents bias. Iterate and improve during the process. Like code, documentation should evolve over time. Solicit feedback from users and regularly review its clarity and accuracy. Consistency across documentation makes it easier to write and read. Standardized templates also reduce the cognitive load on contributors.

Modern tools like Markdown editors, documentation generators, and version control systems simplify the process and integrate seamlessly with workflows. It is also essential to wrote for your audience. Tailor the level of detail and tone to the intended audience. Developers, users, and managers have different needs and expectations. Embed examples as you try to pass your message across. Real-world examples and use cases make abstract concepts tangible and actionable. Integration with the code base is essential. Embedding links to documentation within the code, or using tools like Javadoc or Sphinx, ensures that developers can easily reference relevant materials.

The benefits of investing in high-quality documentation extend far beyond immediate convenience. Over time, it transforms teams, projects, and organizations in profound ways. Developers spend less time deciphering systems and more time solving meaningful problems. Knowledge is no longer confined to a few individuals, reducing bottlenecks. Clear documentation fosters better communication and alignment across teams, particularly in distributed or cross-functional environments. By capturing institutional knowledge, documentation mitigates the impact of employee turnover or project transitions. A thorough understanding of the system allows developers to make informed decisions, avoid duplication of effort, and catch potential issues early. Well-documented systems are easier to maintain, scale, and evolve, ensuring that technical debt does not accumulate unchecked.

Mentorship is another powerful way to encourage knowledge sharing. When senior engineers take the time to mentor junior developers, they not only transfer technical skills but also share their thought processes, decision-making strategies, and approaches to problem-solving. Mentorship relationships often extend beyond technical expertise, helping mentees navigate the complexities of their roles and the organization. For mentors, the act of teaching reinforces their own understanding and sharpens their ability to communicate complex ideas clearly. A mentorship-driven approach to knowledge sharing has a profound impact on the growth and confidence of all participants.

Knowledge sharing doesn't always have to be formal. Informal interactions, such as casual conversations, pair programming, or even coffee breaks, often lead to the most meaningful exchanges. These moments allow engineers to share insights in a low-pressure setting and create bonds that strengthen collaboration. Teams that encourage informal knowledge sharing often find that it fosters creativity and innovation, as individuals feel more comfortable exploring new ideas and seeking diverse perspectives.

One of the most valuable outcomes of a knowledge-sharing culture is the reduction of bottlenecks and dependencies. When knowledge resides with only a few individuals, projects become vulnerable to delays and disruptions if those key contributors are unavailable. By actively sharing information, teams distribute expertise across multiple members, ensuring that no single point of failure exists. This redundancy is particularly important in critical systems, where downtime or errors can have significant consequences. Moreover, sharing knowledge empowers team members to take ownership of their work and contribute to areas beyond their immediate expertise, fostering a sense of shared responsibility.

It also plays a critical role in driving innovation. In environments where information flows freely, individuals can build upon each other's ideas, leading to solutions that no single person could have developed alone. Collaborative brainstorming sessions, hackathons, and cross-functional projects are examples of how knowledge sharing can spark creativity and lead to breakthroughs. By combining diverse perspectives, teams can challenge assumptions, identify new opportunities, and solve problems more effectively. An often-overlooked aspect is its impact on morale and job satisfaction. Engineers who feel that their contributions are valued and that they have access to the resources they need are more likely to be engaged and motivated. A culture that prioritizes learning and growth fosters a sense of purpose, as individuals see their efforts contributing to the team's success and the organization's goals. This sense of fulfillment not only improves retention but also attracts top talent, as skilled professionals are drawn to environments where they can continue to develop and thrive.

Leaders play a pivotal role in fostering a knowledge-sharing culture. By modeling the behavior, they want to see, leaders set the tone for the rest of the team. When managers and senior engineers actively participate in activities that promote this approach, such as giving presentations, writing documentation, or mentoring others, they demonstrate that these practices are valued and expected. Recognition and rewards for individuals who contribute to knowledge sharing further reinforce its importance. Whether it's through public acknowledgment, career growth opportunities, or tangible benefits, celebrating those who share knowledge motivates others to follow suit.

Organizations that prioritize knowledge sharing often see benefits that extend beyond their immediate teams. Shared knowledge creates a more agile organization, better equipped to adapt to changing markets, technologies, and customer needs. It also enhances the organization's reputation, as it becomes known for fostering collaboration and innovation. For example, many companies encourage their engineers to contribute to open-source projects or publish technical blogs, showcasing their expertise and building goodwill within the broader tech community.

Despite its many advantages, fostering this culture requires ongoing effort and commitment. It's not a one-time initiative but a continuous process that evolves with the team and the organization. As teams grow and change, new challenges and opportunities for knowledge sharing will arise, requiring leaders to adapt their strategies and approaches. By maintaining a focus on trust, collaboration, and growth, organizations can create an enduring culture that empowers their engineers and drives long-term success. In the world of software engineering, where the only constant is change, the ability to share knowledge effectively is an invaluable asset. It transforms teams from collections of individuals into cohesive units capable of tackling any challenge. By fostering a culture of openness, trust, and collaboration, engineers and organizations alike can unlock their full potential and leave a legacy of innovation and excellence.

Leaving a legacy as a software engineer involves more than writing efficient code or delivering successful projects. While these achievements are important, a true legacy extends beyond the immediate and tangible outputs of one's work. It lives on in the systems that continue to function, the knowledge shared, and the influence on colleagues and future generations of engineers. At the heart of this legacy is a commitment to documentation, mentorship, and creating systems that endure. Great engineers understand that their work is not just about solving problems today but about enabling others to solve problems tomorrow.

Documentation is one of the most enduring ways an engineer can leave a mark. It is a direct conduit through which knowledge and intent are preserved. Systems inevitably outlast the engineers who build them, and without clear documentation, even the most elegant code can become impenetrable. Future developers must rely on documentation to understand the why behind a system's design choices and its evolution over time. A system built without this foundation becomes a burden to maintain, leading to inefficiency and frustration. But when an engineer leaves behind thorough, well-structured documentation, they provide future teams with the tools to extend, refactor, or rebuild with confidence.

The act and process of documenting is more than just a technical exercise; it is a form of storytelling. Each system has a narrative that is a set of problems, constraints, and decisions that shaped its development. When engineers document their work, they tell this story in a way that others can understand and learn from. This narrative perspective allows those who come after to see the system not as a monolith but as a living thing shaped by the context in which it was created. By embedding this understanding into their documentation, engineers ensure that their systems remain adaptable and relevant, even as technology and organizational needs evolve.

Beyond documentation, mentorship is one of the most powerful ways an engineer can leave a legacy. Mentorship is an act of investment in the people around you, a way of transferring not only technical skills but also values, practices, and wisdom. Engineers who mentor others contribute to the growth of their colleagues in ways that ripple outward, affecting teams, organizations, and even the industry as a whole. A mentor's influence is seen in the mentees who go on to lead projects, innovate solutions, and mentor others in turn. This chain of knowledge and inspiration becomes a living legacy that far outlasts any single individual.

As earlier mentioned, mentorship is not confined to formal relationships. It occurs in everyday interactions, from reviewing code to discussing design decisions. Every opportunity to teach, guide, or provide constructive feedback is a chance to mentor. Engineers who approach their work with a spirit of generosity by sharing their insights and encouraging others create a culture where everyone learns and grows. In such environments, the success of the team is amplified, as each member benefits from the collective expertise and support.

Engineers who leave a legacy also think deeply about the systems they create. They recognize that every line of code, every architectural decision, has implications for the future. Systems designed with clarity, modularity, and scalability in mind are easier to maintain and evolve. These engineers approach their work with humility, understanding that they cannot predict every future requirement but striving to make their systems as adaptable as possible. They document their reasoning, acknowledge trade-offs, and build with empathy for the developers who will follow.

Empathy is a defining trait of engineers who leave a legacy. It manifests in small but meaningful actions: writing code that is easy to read, leaving comments that explain intent, and choosing tools that simplify others' work. Empathy extends beyond technical considerations to include the human side of engineering. Legacy-minded engineers consider the workloads and stress levels of their teams, advocating for sustainable practices and promoting a culture of balance. By prioritizing the well-being of their colleagues, they ensure that their contributions are not just effective but also sustainable. Sharing knowledge outside the immediate team is another way to create a lasting impact. Engineers who write blogs, speak at conferences, or contribute to open-source projects extend their influence beyond the boundaries of their organization. These activities allow others to learn from their experiences, fostering a broader culture of collaboration and innovation. Open-source contributions, in particular, embody the idea of leaving a legacy. By contributing to tools and libraries used by developers worldwide, engineers enable countless others to build and innovate.

The impact of leaving a legacy is not always visible at the moment. It often becomes evident only over time, as systems continue to operate smoothly, teams grow more effectively, and ideas propagate through the industry. Engineers who prioritize legacy may never see the full extent of their influence, but their work sets the stage for others to succeed. They create a foundation upon which new solutions can be built, ensuring that their contributions continue to generate value long after they have moved on.

Legacy-minded engineers also inspire others to think about the future. By demonstrating the importance of documentation, mentorship, and sustainable practices, they encourage their colleagues to adopt similar approaches. This creates a ripple effect, as more engineers begin to think about the long-term impact of their work. Organizations that foster this mindset benefit from a culture of foresight and resilience, where teams are not just focused on immediate goals but also on building for the future.

Ultimately, leaving a legacy is about making choices that prioritize the collective good over individual recognition. It is about thinking beyond immediate deliverables and considering how one's work will affect others, your colleagues, future developers, and even end-users. It is about creating systems, processes, and relationships that endure, empowering others to succeed long after the original work is complete. In this way, the legacy of a great engineer is not measured by the lines of code they write or the projects they deliver but by the lasting impact they have on people and organizations.

CHAPTER EIGHT
Embracing the Unknown: Navigating Uncertainty in Software Development

Ambiguity is an inescapable aspect of software development, and learning to navigate it effectively is a hallmark of successful engineers. Unlike disciplines where processes are rigid and outcomes predictable, software engineering thrives in a space of creativity and exploration, where uncertainty is often the norm. Requirements evolve, technologies shift, and customer needs change. For those unprepared, this ambiguity can be overwhelming, but for those who embrace it, it becomes an opportunity to innovate, grow, and create lasting impact.

Most times ambiguity in software development stems from the dynamic nature of the problems being solved. Many projects begin with only a vague understanding of the desired outcome. A client may articulate a vision without clear specifics, or a team might be tasked with exploring uncharted technical territory. In such situations, engineers are not simply implementers of predefined solutions but rather explorers seeking to define the problem as they develop its solution. This dual challenge of defining and solving simultaneously can be daunting, but it also enables immense creativity and adaptability.

One of the keys to thriving in ambiguous situations is developing a mindset that embraces uncertainty as a natural part of the process. This mindset starts with accepting that not all answers will be available at the outset. Engineers who resist this reality often waste valuable time seeking perfect clarity, while those who lean into ambiguity approach the task with curiosity and flexibility. They understand that part of their role is to bring structure to the undefined, carving clarity from chaos one step at a time. This ability to start moving without all the answers is a skill that grows with experience but can also be nurtured intentionally.

Communication plays a critical role in managing ambiguity. When requirements are unclear, effective communication helps ensure that all stakeholders share a mutual understanding of the situation. Engineers who are adept at asking the right questions can uncover hidden assumptions, surface constraints, and identify priorities. They approach discussions with a problem-solving mindset, seeking to align diverse perspectives and clarify goals. This process often requires repeated conversations, as stakeholders themselves may need time to refine their vision. Patience and persistence in these dialogues are essential, as rushing to conclusions can lead to misaligned expectations and wasted effort.

Ambiguity also demands a balance between flexibility and decisiveness. Engineers must be willing to adapt as new information emerges, but they also need to make decisions based on the best available data. Prolonged indecision in the face of uncertainty can paralyze progress, while premature choices may lead to suboptimal outcomes. The most effective engineers find a middle ground, taking calculated risks when necessary and revisiting decisions as new insights come to light. They view mistakes not as failures but as opportunities to learn and iterate, cultivating resilience and confidence in the face of the unknown.

It often pushes engineers to rely on their instincts and creativity. With no clear roadmap to follow, they must draw on their technical expertise, problem-solving skills, and understanding of user needs to propose solutions. This process can feel like navigating in the dark, but it also opens the door to innovative thinking. Without rigid constraints, engineers are free to experiment, explore unconventional ideas, and discover novel approaches. The best solutions often arise not from adhering to a predetermined plan but from the iterative process of testing, learning, and refining in response to the evolving situation.

One of the challenges of working in ambiguous conditions is managing the emotional toll it can take. Uncertainty can be stressful, especially for engineers who prefer well-defined tasks and clear outcomes. The pressure to deliver results despite incomplete information can lead to frustration, self-doubt, and burnout.

Addressing these challenges requires cultivating a sense of psychological safety within teams. When individuals feel supported, valued, and encouraged to share their concerns, they are better equipped to cope with ambiguity. Leaders play a crucial role in fostering this environment by modeling transparency, acknowledging uncertainties, and providing reassurance.

Ambiguity is also an opportunity for growth. Professionals who navigate uncertain situations develop valuable skills that extend beyond technical expertise. They learn to think critically, communicate effectively, and make decisions under pressure. These experiences build confidence and prepare them to tackle increasingly complex challenges in the future. Over time, engineers who embrace ambiguity become more comfortable with uncertainty, viewing it not as a threat but as an integral part of their work. They become leaders who can guide others through uncharted territory, inspiring confidence and collaboration even in the most unpredictable circumstances.

These examples illustrate how ambiguity can lead to both challenges and opportunities. Consider a project where a team is tasked with building a product for an emerging market. At the outset, the target audience may be poorly defined, the desired features unclear, and the technical requirements unknown. Rather than waiting for perfect clarity, the team begins by conducting user research, prototyping potential solutions, and gathering feedback. Each iteration brings new insights, gradually shaping the product into something that meets user needs. Along the way, the team encounters unexpected obstacles, technical limitations, shifting market trends, or conflicting stakeholder priorities but their willingness to adapt allows them to overcome these hurdles and deliver a successful outcome. Another example is the adoption of an efficient technology with limited documentation or community support. Engineers working with such tools often face a steep learning curve and an abundance of unknowns. However, by experimenting, sharing discoveries, and collaborating with peers, they can unlock the potential of the technology and pave the way for others to follow. These pioneers embrace ambiguity not as a barrier but as an opportunity to innovate and lead.

Thriving in ambiguity also requires a sense of purpose. Engineers who understand the broader impact of their work are more motivated to persevere through uncertainty. They see their efforts as part of a larger mission whether they're improving lives through technology, advancing knowledge, or contributing to organizational success. This sense of purpose provides clarity amid confusion, guiding decisions and sustaining momentum when challenges arise. It reminds engineers that ambiguity is not an obstacle to avoiding it but a space where meaningful progress can be made.

This approach is not a flaw in the software development process; it is a feature. It reflects the dynamic and ever-changing nature of technology, markets, and user needs. Engineers who learn to navigate this uncertainty with skill and confidence become invaluable assets to their teams and organizations. They bring clarity to complexity, creativity to constraints, and resilience to challenges. By embracing ambiguity, they unlock new possibilities and drive innovation, leaving a lasting impact on the projects they undertake and the people they work with.

Adapting to new technologies and trends is one of the most defining characteristics of a successful software engineer. The technology landscape is in a constant state of flux, with frameworks, programming languages, tools, and methodologies evolving at a rapid pace. In this environment, stagnation is not an option; those who fail to keep up risk becoming obsolete. However, the ability to adapt to new technologies is not just about survival but it is also an opportunity to thrive, innovate, and lead. For engineers, this adaptability requires a mindset of continuous learning, an openness to experimentation, and the ability to strike a balance between adopting the new and leveraging the familiar.

The sheer pace of technological advancement in the software industry can feel overwhelming. Every year, new tools and frameworks emerge, each promising to revolutionize the way software is built. Engineers are bombarded with buzzwords and trends, from the rise of artificial intelligence and machine learning to the rapid adoption of serverless computing and blockchain technologies. Keeping up with these developments requires a deliberate and strategic approach. Engineers must cultivate an ability to discern which trends are worth investing time in and which are unlikely to deliver long-term value.

This discernment often comes with experience but can also be honed through active engagement with the tech community, attending conferences, reading blogs, and participating in forums where emerging technologies are discussed.

One of the most significant challenges professionals faces when adapting to new technologies is the learning curve. Mastering a new tool or framework takes time and effort, and this can be daunting, particularly when deadlines loom or project demands are high. However, the best engineers view these challenges as opportunities rather than obstacles. They approach learning with curiosity and persistence, seeking out resources such as tutorials, documentation, and courses to build their understanding. They also recognize the value of hands-on experimentation, knowing that true mastery comes not just from studying but from applying new knowledge in practical scenarios. By creating small side projects, contributing to open-source initiatives, or even experimenting with new tools within the context of existing projects, engineers can accelerate their learning and gain confidence in using new technologies.

Experimentation plays a crucial role in adapting to new tools and processes. Unlike well-established tools, which often come with extensive documentation and a wealth of community knowledge, emerging technologies can be uncharted territory. Professionals who are willing to explore these tools without fear of failure often discover creative ways to solve problems and gain a competitive edge. Experimentation allows them to understand the strengths and limitations of a technology, identify its potential use cases, and determine whether it aligns with the needs of their team or organization. This willingness to experiment is not about recklessness but about taking calculated risks, learning from mistakes, and iterating toward better solutions.

One of the keys to successfully adapting is collaboration. The process of learning and implementing new tools is often more effective when done as a team. Collaboration allows engineers to share insights, divide the workload of researching and experimenting, and learn from one another's experiences. Pair programming, knowledge-sharing sessions, and collaborative problem-solving are all ways to ensure that the benefits of new technologies are realized collectively. Moreover, involving the entire team in the adoption process ensures that everyone feels invested in the change and reduces resistance to new approaches.

While the benefits of adopting new technologies can be significant, it is equally important to approach them with caution. Not every new tool or framework is a good fit for every project, and chasing the latest trends without careful consideration can lead to unnecessary complexity and wasted resources. Engineers must evaluate new technologies against a set of criteria, including their maturity, community support, compatibility with existing systems, and alignment with project goals. This evaluation process requires a balance of technical expertise and strategic thinking. By focusing on the long-term impact of their choices, engineers can avoid the pitfalls of shiny object syndrome and make decisions that deliver lasting value.

Mastering these new processes also requires resilience. The process of learning and integrating a new tool is rarely smooth; challenges are inevitable, from debugging unexpected issues to navigating sparse or incomplete documentation. Engineers who succeed in this environment are those who persevere, maintaining a positive attitude and a problem-solving mindset. They view setbacks as part of the learning process and use them as opportunities to deepen their understanding. This resilience not only helps them overcome immediate obstacles but also builds confidence for future challenges.

The ability to adapt to new technologies is not just a technical skill but also a mindset. It requires a willingness to embrace change and recognition that growth often involves discomfort. Individuals who adopt this mindset are more likely to seek out opportunities for learning, even when it means stepping outside their comfort zones. They understand that their value lies not in their mastery of a specific tool but in their ability to learn, unlearn, and relearn as the industry evolves. This adaptability makes them versatile and resilient, qualities that are highly prized in the fast-moving world of software development. Adopting new technologies often has a ripple effect, influencing not only the people who implement them but also the teams, organizations, and users they serve. When new tools are chosen thoughtfully and integrated effectively, they can lead to significant improvements in productivity, performance, and user satisfaction. For example, a team that adopts a modern development framework may find that it accelerates their ability to deliver features, reduces the complexity of maintaining their operations, and improves the overall quality of their software. Similarly, adopting advanced analytics tools or machine learning models can unlock new capabilities, enabling organizations to make data-driven decisions or deliver personalized experiences to users.

However, the decision to adopt new technologies must always be guided by the needs of the project and the organization. Professionals must resist the temptation to adopt tools simply because they are popular or because they offer a marginal improvement over existing solutions. Instead, they should focus on solving real problems and delivering tangible benefits. This disciplined approach ensures that the adoption of new technologies serves a purpose and adds value rather than creating unnecessary disruption.

This also presents an opportunity for leadership. Engineers who take the initiative to learn and advocate for new tools can become catalysts for positive change within their organizations. By sharing their knowledge, mentoring others, and demonstrating the value of new approaches, they inspire their teams to embrace innovation and strive for excellence. This leadership extends beyond technical expertise; it is about fostering a culture of curiosity, collaboration, and continuous improvement. Engineers who lead by example in adapting to new technologies leave a lasting impact, not only on their teams but also on the broader industry. The process of adapting to new technologies is not without its challenges, but it is also one of the most rewarding aspects of a software engineer's career. It keeps the work exciting, offering endless opportunities to learn, grow, and push the boundaries of what is possible. For engineers who embrace this journey, the rewards go beyond technical proficiency as they gain a deeper understanding of the industry, a broader perspective on problem-solving, and the confidence to tackle whatever comes next. In a field defined by change, the ability to adapt is not just a skill but a way of thriving in an ever-evolving world.

Thriving under pressure is a critical skill for software engineers, as the nature of the work often involves tight deadlines, high expectations, and evolving priorities. The fast-paced environment of software development demands a blend of technical expertise, emotional resilience, and effective teamwork. Engineers who learn to navigate these challenges not only succeed in their roles but also contribute to creating a culture of excellence and collaboration. Thriving under pressure does not mean avoiding stress altogether; rather, it involves managing it effectively, maintaining focus, and finding opportunities for growth in the midst of adversity.

A very common source of pressure in software development is the ever-present reality of deadlines. Whether it is a product launch, a client deliverable, or an internal milestone, deadlines create urgency and demand efficiency. While deadlines can be motivating, they can also lead to significant stress if not managed carefully. Engineers who thrive under such conditions approach deadlines with a strategic mindset. They break down complex tasks into manageable steps, prioritize effectively, and maintain a clear focus on the end goal. This structured approach allows them to make steady progress, even when the timeline feels overwhelming.

Time management is an essential skill for thriving under pressure. Individuals who are adept at managing their time know how to allocate their energy and attention to the most critical tasks. They understand the importance of setting boundaries, avoiding distractions, and saying no to unnecessary requests. By protecting their time, they create space to focus on deep work and problem-solving, which are essential for delivering high-quality results under tight deadlines. Additionally, effective time management involves recognizing when to ask for help or delegate tasks, ensuring that the workload is distributed fairly across the team.

Pressure often amplifies the importance of communication. In high-stakes situations, clear and consistent communication becomes a lifeline for teams. Engineers who excel under pressure know how to articulate their progress, flag potential roadblocks, and provide updates in a way that keeps stakeholders informed and aligned. They foster open lines of communication within their teams, creating an environment where concerns can be raised and addressed without fear of judgment. This transparency reduces misunderstandings, builds trust, and enables teams to respond quickly to changing circumstances. Collaboration is another cornerstone of thriving under pressure. Software development is rarely a solo endeavor, and the ability to work effectively with others is crucial when deadlines loom or priorities shift. Engineers who thrive in these situations leverage the strengths of their teammates, pooling their collective knowledge and expertise to solve problems efficiently. They create a sense of camaraderie, encouraging mutual support and celebrating small wins along the way. This collaborative spirit not only improves outcomes but also makes the process more enjoyable, even in challenging times.

Resilience is perhaps the most important quality for engineers facing pressure. It is the ability to bounce back from setbacks, adapt to changing conditions, and maintain a positive outlook despite difficulties. Engineers who are resilient view challenges as opportunities to learn and grow. They embrace the iterative nature of software development, recognizing that mistakes and failures are part of the process. Rather than dwelling on what went wrong, they focus on finding solutions and moving forward. This mindset not only helps them cope with immediate pressures but also builds confidence in future challenges.

Emotional intelligence plays a significant role in resilience. Engineers who are emotionally intelligent are better equipped to manage their own stress and support their teammates. They practice self-awareness, recognizing when they are feeling overwhelmed and taking steps to regain their composure. They also demonstrate empathy, understanding the pressures their colleagues are facing and offering encouragement or assistance as needed. This emotional intelligence fosters a sense of connection and teamwork, which is vital for thriving under pressure.

Another factor that enables engineers to excel under pressure is a sense of purpose. When engineers understand the broader impact of their work, they are more motivated to persevere through challenges. This sense of purpose provides clarity and direction, helping them prioritize their efforts and stay focused on what matters most. It also serves as a source of inspiration, reminding them that their work contributes to something larger than themselves. Whether it is improving user experiences, solving complex problems, or advancing technology, this sense of purpose can be a powerful antidote to stress.

It is also essential to note that in high-pressure situations, engineers must also be mindful of their physical and mental well-being. Long hours, tight deadlines, and intense workloads can take a toll on health if not managed carefully. Engineers who thrive under pressure prioritize self-care, ensuring they get enough sleep, eat well, and take breaks when needed. They understand that maintaining their health is not a luxury but a necessity for sustained performance. Additionally, they develop coping strategies for managing stress, such as practicing mindfulness, engaging in physical activity, or seeking support from friends and colleagues. These practices help them stay grounded and maintain their energy and focus during challenging times.

Leadership plays a crucial role in helping teams thrive under pressure. Effective leaders provide clear direction, set realistic expectations, and offer support to their teams. They create an environment of psychological safety, where individuals feel empowered to take risks, ask questions, and voice concerns. Leaders who model resilience and composure set the tone for their teams, demonstrating that it is possible to navigate pressure with grace and determination. By fostering a positive and supportive culture, they enable their teams to excel even in the most demanding circumstances.

Thriving under pressure is not about being immune to stress but about developing the skills, mindset, and habits to manage it effectively. Engineers who excel in these situations understand that pressure is an inherent part of their work and that it can be a catalyst for growth and innovation. By embracing challenges, collaborating with others, and maintaining a sense of purpose, they turn pressure into an opportunity to achieve excellence. Their ability to thrive under pressure not only benefits their own careers but also contributes to the success of their teams, projects, and organizations.

CHAPTER NINE
The Craft of Mentorship: Giving Back and Growing Through Teaching

Throughout my career, the role of a mentee has been pivotal in shaping who I am today. Being mentored by experienced professionals has provided me with invaluable insights, guidance, and perspectives that I would not have acquired on my own. The process of learning from someone who has walked the path before me has not only accelerated my growth but has also taught me how to navigate the often complex and ever-changing landscape of the software engineering world. The relationship between mentor and mentee is one of mutual respect, trust, and shared purpose. As a mentee, I have learned that the value of mentorship is not just in receiving advice, but in gaining a deeper understanding of myself, my goals, and the broader context in which I work.

When I reflect on my journey as a mentee, the first thing that stands out is the sheer importance of guidance. In the early stages of my career, the challenges I faced seemed insurmountable at times. I was thrust into situations where I had to quickly adapt to new technologies, work under tight deadlines, and meet the high expectations of clients and stakeholders. Without the steady support of mentors, it would have been easy to feel overwhelmed or discouraged. However, having someone to turn to for advice made all the difference. They provided me with a roadmap, helping me avoid common pitfalls and showing me how to approach problems with confidence and clarity.

The impact of a mentor is most noticeable when I encounter challenges that feel like they might derail my progress. In the software industry, these moments are inevitable. Projects don't always go as planned, deadlines are missed, and the code doesn't work as expected. In these moments, having a mentor who can offer both technical advice and emotional support can be a game-changer. My mentors taught me that failure is not something to fear but an essential part of growth. They helped me reframe setbacks as opportunities to learn rather than as obstacles to my success. This shift in mindset has been invaluable, and it has helped me approach every challenge, no matter how difficult, with resilience and optimism.

Another lesson I learned from my mentors is the importance of asking questions. Early in my career, I was hesitant to seek help, fearing that doing so would make me appear incompetent. However, my mentors made it clear that asking questions was not a sign of weakness but of strength. By seeking out answers, I not only gained a better understanding of the task at hand but also developed the critical thinking skills necessary to solve complex problems independently. This lesson has stayed with me throughout my career, and I have since adopted the philosophy that there is no such thing as a "dumb" question. Mentorship taught me that the act of asking questions is an essential part of learning and growth, and it has enabled me to become a more effective engineer.

In addition to technical guidance, mentors also provided me with broader life lessons that have had a profound impact on my career. They taught me the importance of work-life balance, the need to set boundaries, and the value of taking care of my mental and physical health. In the fast-paced world of software development, it is easy to become consumed by the work, but my mentors showed me that maintaining a healthy balance is crucial for long-term success. They encouraged me to take time for myself, pursue hobbies outside of work, and spend time with loved ones. These lessons have helped me avoid burnout and maintain a sense of perspective, even during the most challenging periods of my career.

The most impactful seniors I had were those who took a genuine interest in my personal and professional growth. They didn't just offer advice in a one-sided manner; they took the time to understand my strengths, weaknesses, and aspirations. They listened to my concerns, encouraged me to pursue my goals, and provided constructive feedback that helped me improve. This personalized approach made me feel valued and supported, and it instilled in me a sense of confidence and self-belief that has been crucial to my success. When mentors take the time to build a relationship with their mentees, the learning experience becomes far more meaningful and impactful. One of the key aspects of the relationship that I came to appreciate was the role of constructive feedback. As a mentee, it is easy to become attached to one's ideas and solutions, but my mentors showed me the importance of being open to feedback and willing to adapt. They taught me how to view feedback as a tool for improvement rather than as criticism. This mindset shift allowed me to receive constructive criticism without taking it personally and instead use it to refine my skills and become a better engineer. Moreover, my mentors were never harsh or dismissive in their feedback; they always offered it in a way that was supportive and motivating, helping me to feel empowered to grow rather than discouraged.

Over time, I came to realize that mentorship is not a one-time event but a continuous process. Even as I gained more experience and knowledge, my mentors remained a valuable source of guidance. They provided ongoing support, helping me navigate the changing landscape of the software industry. As technology evolved, they encouraged me to stay current with new trends and tools, reminding me that learning is a lifelong process. This emphasis on continuous learning has been one of the most important lessons I have carried forward in my career. These individuals taught me that the key to success in software engineering is not only technical skill but also the ability to adapt and grow throughout one's career.

The role of mentorship in my career has been transformative. It has not only shaped my technical abilities but also influenced my approach to problem-solving, collaboration, and personal development. Through my mentors, I learned how to navigate challenges with resilience, seek out answers when needed, and embrace the importance of continuous learning. Moreover, the guidance and support I received helped me build the confidence I needed to take on larger responsibilities, make difficult decisions, and grow into a leadership role. The value of having someone to turn to during the early stages of my career cannot be overstated, and it has had a lasting impact on both my professional and personal growth.

Perhaps the most meaningful aspect is the sense of connection it fosters. It is about building relationships based on trust, respect, and shared experience. My mentors provided not only technical advice but also a sense of belonging and community. In a field as fast paced and ever-changing as software engineering, it can sometimes feel isolating, especially when faced with difficult challenges. However, the support and encouragement of my seniors and experts reminded me that I was never alone. This sense of connection has been instrumental in helping me persevere through tough times and continue striving toward my goals.

The experiences I had as a mentee have been integral to shaping my values and approach as a mentor. I have learned that the most important role of a mentor is to support, encourage, and empower others to reach their full potential. The lessons I received from my mentors have become the foundation of the mentorship I offer to others, and it has become clear to me that the act of giving back is not only fulfilling but essential for my continued growth. Just as my mentors helped me navigate challenges and develop my skills, I now have the opportunity to do the same for others, passing on the knowledge and wisdom I have gained over the years.

Being mentored has taught me the value of humility, the importance of learning from others, and the strength that comes from collaboration. It has shown me that no one achieves success in isolation, and that mentorship is a powerful way to give back to the community while simultaneously growing as a professional. As I reflect on my journey, I am deeply grateful to the mentors who have shaped my career, and I carry the lessons they imparted with me every day. Their impact on my life cannot be overstated, and I strive to honor their guidance by mentoring others and paying forward the wisdom they shared with me.

As my career progressed, I transitioned from being a mentee to becoming a mentor myself. This shift marked a significant turning point in my professional development, as it required me to look beyond my own growth and focus on helping others succeed. Being a mentor has been a deeply rewarding experience, one that has allowed me to both share the knowledge I have accumulated over the years and also deepen my own understanding of the subjects I thought I had mastered. Teaching others, guiding them through their challenges, and celebrating their successes has been an incredibly fulfilling aspect of my career.

The first realization I had as I took on the role of teaching and grooming others was the immense responsibility it carries. Mentoring is not simply about providing answers to problems; it is about helping someone develop the skills and confidence to find their own solutions. As a mentor, I was no longer just responsible for my own work but for helping another individual navigate the complexities of their career. I quickly learned that the process requires patience, empathy, and the ability to see the bigger picture. A mentor's influence can shape a mentee's approach to problem-solving, their work ethic, and even their career trajectory. Recognizing the weight of this responsibility made me approach mentoring with a great deal of care and intentionality.

One of the most valuable aspects of these aspects is that it provides an opportunity for reflection. When you teach someone else, you are forced to articulate your own thought process, to break down complex concepts into digestible pieces, and to question your own assumptions. I often found that explaining a solution to a mentee required me to revisit the core principles behind it, which, in turn, deepened my understanding. Mentoring became a process of continuous learning, where I not only helped others solve problems but also reinforced my own knowledge and skill set. It reminded me that knowledge is not static; it evolves as we teach and learn from each other.

At first, I struggled with the challenge of balancing the technical demands of my own work with the time and energy required to support my mentees. As the one leading these individuals, I had to ensure that I was available to answer questions, provide feedback, and guide my mentees through their learning processes. This often meant carving out time during busy workdays to meet with them, review their code, or discuss their progress. The process of mentoring required me to be organized and efficient with my time. I had to learn to manage multiple priorities effectively, ensuring that both my mentees and my own projects received the attention they deserved.

Over time, I realized that the process is not just about technical skills but also about personal growth and development. Many of the challenges faced by my mentees were not purely technical; they often involved navigating workplace dynamics, managing time effectively, or building self-confidence. In these instances, I found that mentoring required me to wear many hats: a coach, a counselor, and sometimes even a cheerleader. I had to help my mentees develop not just as engineers but as professionals capable of thriving in a competitive and ever-changing industry. I encouraged them to set clear goals, to stay adaptable, and to seek out opportunities for growth. I also emphasized the importance of learning from failure and embracing it as an essential part of their development. In my experience, the ability to bounce back from setbacks is one of the most important qualities for success in software engineering, and I made it a point to instill that belief in my mentees.

Effective mentorship also requires the ability to give constructive feedback in a way that is both honest and supportive. It is easy to point out flaws, but a good mentor also helps the mentee understand how to improve. I learned that feedback should be specific, actionable, and framed in a way that encourages growth. I always tried to highlight what my mentees did well before offering suggestions for improvement, creating an environment where they felt motivated to continue learning rather than discouraged. In some cases, this feedback also required me to be vulnerable, admitting that I, too, had made mistakes and learned from them. This helped create a sense of mutual respect and trust between me and my mentees, as they saw that I wasn't just lecturing them from a place of authority but rather sharing experiences from my own journey.

I must confess that one of the most fulfilling aspects of mentoring is seeing someone grow in their confidence and abilities. Watching a person go from struggling with a particular concept to mastering it and applying it independently is incredibly gratifying. It is a testament to the power of guidance and support, and it reinforces the idea that mentorship is a two-way relationship. As a mentor, I had the privilege of being part of their journey, providing the encouragement and advice they needed to succeed. But ultimately, the credit belongs to the mentee for their hard work, determination, and willingness to learn. It was always a proud moment when a mentee completed a project or solved a particularly difficult problem, knowing that I had played a role in their success.

The growth I witnessed in these professionals I have had the opportunity to groom also had a profound impact on me. It made me realize that mentoring is not a one-way street; it is a reciprocal process. While I was helping my mentees grow in their careers, they were helping me grow as well. They challenged me to think differently, introduced me to new perspectives, and forced me to reconsider my approaches to problem-solving. In many ways, this kept me humble and reminded me that there is always something new to learn, regardless of how experienced we become. It reinforced the idea that we never stop being students of our craft, and that teaching others is one of the most effective ways to continue growing.

Another key aspect of mentoring that became apparent over time is the importance of adaptability. Each mentee is different, and each brings their own strengths, weaknesses, and learning styles to the table. As a mentor, it was essential for me to tailor my approach to fit the unique needs of each individual. Some persons needed more guidance and reassurance, while others thrived on independence and self-direction. Some preferred hands-on learning through coding exercises, while others benefited more from discussions and brainstorming sessions. Recognizing these differences and adapting my mentoring style accordingly allowed me to be more effective and to foster a learning environment that was both supportive and challenging. The ability to adjust my approach to each mentee's needs was one of the most rewarding aspects of helping them grow, as it allowed me to help them achieve their goals in the most effective way possible.

As I became more experienced as a mentor, I also began to see the broader impact of mentorship on the team and organization as a whole. This process is not just an individual activity; it contributes to building a culture of learning and collaboration within a team. When engineers mentor others, they are not only helping the mentee but also raising the overall competency and morale of the team. A strong mentoring culture fosters a sense of community, where knowledge is shared freely, and everyone is committed to each other's success. It also promotes a growth mindset within the organization, encouraging employees to continuously improve their skills and seek out new opportunities for development. This, in turn, helps create a more innovative and productive environment where people feel valued and motivated to contribute their best work.

It is also a key tool for retaining talent. By investing in the development of junior engineers and providing them with the support and guidance they need, organizations can ensure that their most promising employees stay and grow within the company. Mentorship helps create a sense of belonging and purpose, which is essential for employee satisfaction and retention. It also helps develop future leaders within the organization, ensuring a continuous pipeline of talent and expertise. As a mentor, I have always made it a priority to help my mentees develop not just technical skills but also leadership qualities, as I believe this is crucial for their long-term success.

Honestly, transitioning from being a mentee to a mentor has been one of the most transformative experiences of my career. It has taught me that mentorship is not just about sharing knowledge; it is about creating an environment where both mentor and mentee can learn, grow, and thrive together. It has deepened my understanding of software engineering, honed my communication and leadership skills, and reinforced my passion for continuous learning. The most rewarding aspect is seeing others succeed and knowing that I played a small part in helping them reach their potential. As I continue in my career, I am committed to mentoring others and giving back to the community that has helped me along the way. Mentorship is a craft, one that requires dedication, patience, and empathy, but it is also one of the most fulfilling and impactful aspects of being a software engineer.

Its benefits are tremendous and far reaching. It is a powerful force that extends far beyond individual growth and development. It has the potential to shape entire teams, organizations, and even the broader software engineering community. As I reflect on my journey as both a mentor and a mentee, I am increasingly aware of how mentorship can foster a culture of learning, collaboration, and mutual support. It is a cornerstone for building long-term, sustainable success not just for individuals but for organizations as a whole. The ripple effect of mentorship can transform teams, create environments where innovation thrives, and help build legacies that endure long after the initial guidance has been given.

The primary way in which mentorship contributes to organizational culture is by promoting a learning environment. In the fast-paced, constant change in the field of software engineering, staying ahead of the curve is crucial. Technology evolves quickly, and staying relevant means constantly acquiring new skills, adapting to new tools, and understanding emerging trends. When mentorship is embedded in the culture of an organization, it helps ensure that learning never stops. Teams that are actively involved in mentoring each other create a space where knowledge flows freely, and everyone, from the most experienced engineers to the newest recruits, feels empowered to share what they know. This constant exchange of ideas and experiences fosters an environment of continuous improvement, which is essential for long-term success in a rapidly evolving industry.

It also plays a significant role in building trust and cohesion within teams. Trust is the foundation of any successful team, and it is something that must be cultivated intentionally. When mentorship is a priority, team members demonstrate a genuine interest in each other's growth, which naturally leads to stronger relationships and more open communication. As a mentor, you invest time in getting to know your mentees not only as professionals but as individuals. This personal connection can help break down barriers, create a safe space for asking questions, and encourage vulnerability, which is essential for growth. It also strengthens the bonds between team members, making them more likely to collaborate effectively, support one another, and share knowledge and resources. This sense of camaraderie enhances the overall productivity and morale of the team, fostering an environment where everyone feels valued and supported.

A strong mentorship culture can also significantly improve employee retention. In many organizations, the loss of a skilled engineer can be devastating. However, mentorship helps mitigate this risk by providing junior engineers with a sense of belonging and purpose. When engineers are supported and encouraged by mentors, they are more likely to remain in the organization, as they feel valued and see clear opportunities for growth. It creates an environment in which employees feel they are not just cogs in a machine but are part of something larger such as a team, an organization, a community. It gives them a sense of direction and purpose and provides the emotional and professional support necessary to overcome obstacles and pursue their goals. When employees feel they are being invested in and that their development is a priority, they are more likely to remain loyal to the company and invest in its success.

It also plays a critical role in developing future leaders. As I have experienced throughout my career, leadership is not just about technical expertise but also about interpersonal skills, emotional intelligence, and the ability to inspire and motivate others. The best leaders are often those who have had strong mentors themselves, and who understand the value of mentoring others in turn. By providing mentorship, organizations are actively shaping the next generation of leaders. When senior engineers take the time to mentor junior engineers, they are not only helping them grow in their technical abilities but also preparing them for leadership roles. Leadership requires more than just the ability to solve technical problems; it requires empathy, the ability to communicate effectively, and a commitment to helping others grow. It helps develop these skills by encouraging senior engineers to engage with their mentees on a deeper level, offering guidance, support, and feedback that goes beyond technical expertise.

Mentorship also contributes to diversity and inclusion within the software engineering field. The tech industry, like many others, has struggled with issues of representation, particularly when it comes to gender, race, and other underrepresented groups. By fostering a culture of mentorship, organizations can create more opportunities for individuals from diverse backgrounds to succeed. It provides a platform for diverse voices to be heard and for individuals to receive the support they need to excel in a field that may not always been welcoming. It allows for more personalized guidance and support, which can help individuals navigate the challenges they may face as they advance in their careers. As a mentor, I have made it a priority to ensure that my mentees, regardless of their background, feel empowered and equipped to succeed in the industry. By supporting diverse talent, mentorship plays a key role in promoting equity and inclusion within the organization and the broader software engineering community.

Beyond the organizational level, it also has a profound impact on the broader software engineering community. The field of software engineering is built on collaboration and the sharing of knowledge. When engineers mentor others, they contribute to a collective body of knowledge that extends far beyond their own team or company. The more experienced engineers share their insights, lessons learned, and best practices, the more the entire community benefits. This knowledge transfer is essential for driving innovation, solving complex problems, and advancing the field. Mentorship ensures that the lessons learned from one generation of engineers are passed on to the next, allowing the entire industry to grow and improve. In many ways, mentorship is how the software engineering community sustains itself, ensuring that there is a continuous pipeline of talent and knowledge that drives progress.

In my own experience, I have seen the impact of mentorship reach far beyond the immediate mentees I have worked with. When I have taken on a mentee, I've always tried to keep in mind that I am not only helping that individual grow but also contributing to the development of the broader community. Every time I share knowledge with a mentee, I also encouraging them to pass that knowledge on to others. In this way, mentorship becomes a cycle, with each generation of engineers helping the next. This sense of collective responsibility is one of the most powerful aspects of mentorship as it creates a culture where individuals are not just focused on their own success but on the success of the community as a whole.

Ultimately, mentorship is about leaving a legacy. It is about ensuring that the lessons we have learned throughout our careers are passed on to the next generation. The impact of a good mentor lasts long after the relationship has ended, as mentees take the lessons they have learned and apply them to their own work, their own teams, and their own careers. The ripple effect of this mentorship extends far beyond the initial mentor-mentee relationship, creating a culture of learning and growth that benefits everyone in the community. When you invest in someone else's success, you create a lasting impact that can influence not just one individual's career but the trajectory of an entire industry.

For me, the most fulfilling aspect of mentorship has been the opportunity to give back. I have benefited immensely from the mentorship I received early in my career, and it has been a privilege to be able to pass that knowledge on to others. The joy of watching a mentee succeed, knowing that you played a part in their growth, is one of the most rewarding experiences in my career. But mentorship is not just about what I give to others, but it is also about what I receive in return. It challenges me to continue growing, to stay curious, and to always be open to new ideas and perspectives. It has made me a better engineer, a better leader, and a better person.

CHAPTER TEN
The Software Engineer's Lifecycle: Skills, Tools and Mindset

As I look back on my career as a software engineer, one of the most profound realizations I have is how much my skills, mindset, and approach to the field have evolved over the years. From my early days as a junior developer, struggling to get my first lines of code to work, to becoming a senior engineer with the ability to architect complex systems, the transformation has been both gradual and, at times, overwhelming. In the beginning, my focus was almost entirely on acquiring technical skills such as learning languages, mastering frameworks, and getting comfortable with the mechanics of development. However, as time went on, I began to realize that being an effective software engineer is not just about technical competence. It's about how you approach problems, how you interact with colleagues, and how you continue to grow in a field that is constantly evolving.

When I first started as a junior developer, I was primarily concerned with solving immediate problems: debugging code, implementing features, and understanding the requirements laid out by others. The technical knowledge I had at that time was largely based on what I had learned in school and the programming languages I had practiced during personal projects. I was comfortable in a few languages but had limited exposure to the broader ecosystem of tools and techniques used in the industry. It wasn't uncommon for me to get stuck on a bug for hours, only to realize later that a simple change could have solved the problem. At that time, my mindset was focused on getting the job done and learning just enough to meet the immediate needs of the project. There was little consideration of long-term solutions, code quality, or design principles.

During these early years, I struggled with imposter syndrome. I constantly questioned my abilities, comparing myself to more experienced engineers who seemed to have all the answers. The disparity between my limited knowledge and the breadth of experience around me often made me feel inadequate. However, it was also in these moments of uncertainty that I began to learn some of the most valuable lessons about growth. I realized that it was okay not to have all the answers and that asking questions, seeking help, and learning from mistakes were all crucial to my development. I began to recognize that becoming an expert in software engineering wasn't about memorizing syntax or mastering a specific toolset; it was about developing a mindset of continuous learning and resilience.

As I gained more experience, my perspective began to shift. I started paying more attention to the overall design of the systems I was working on, not just the individual features I was building. I realized that writing clean, maintainable code was just as important as writing code that worked. I started to develop an appreciation for software design patterns and principles such as SOLID, and I began to understand the importance of code reviews. Initially, I viewed code reviews as a form of judgment, a reminder of what I didn't know. But over time, I came to understand that they were an invaluable learning opportunity. Through code reviews, I learned how to communicate technical ideas clearly, how to spot potential issues before they become problems, and how to take constructive feedback without taking it personally. This period of growth marked the transition from a junior developer who focused purely on execution to an engineer who began to think critically about how to design, build, and maintain scalable systems.

One of the most significant milestones in my career was learning how to be more intentional about my learning process. As a junior developer, I often felt like I was just trying to keep up, taking in whatever I could as quickly as possible to stay relevant. But as I grew in my role, I realized that I had to be more strategic in my development. I started setting specific learning goals for myself, focusing on areas where I felt weak or areas that I knew would be important for my career progression. This shift in mindset going from reactive learning to proactive learning was a game-changer. I began to focus on not just learning new programming languages, but also understanding architectural concepts, the principles of DevOps, and methodologies like Agile and Scrum. By consciously expanding my knowledge and skills, I was able to approach challenges with more confidence and a deeper understanding of the trade-offs involved in different solutions.

As I moved into more senior roles, my responsibilities began to shift from just writing code to designing systems and guiding the development process. This new phase of my career was a significant challenge, as it required me to think about software engineering in a broader context. It wasn't enough to simply build features; I had to ensure that the systems I designed were scalable, maintainable, and aligned with the company's long-term goals. I also began to take on more leadership responsibilities, mentoring junior engineers, reviewing architectural decisions, and helping to steer the direction of projects. This new level of responsibility required me to balance the technical aspects of development with the interpersonal skills needed to lead teams effectively.

In these roles, I learned that being a senior engineer wasn't about knowing everything; it was about knowing how to make informed decisions and how to facilitate collaboration among different stakeholders. My focus shifted from just solving technical problems to understanding the bigger picture. I began to realize that effective software engineering is not just about writing code but it's about understanding the needs of the business, working with product managers, collaborating with designers, and ensuring that the engineering team was aligned with the company's strategic goals. This broader perspective helped me approach problems from different angles, considering not just the technical feasibility of a solution, but also its impact on the business and its long-term sustainability.

Perhaps one of the most challenging yet rewarding parts of my career has been learning to adapt to the constantly changing landscape of software engineering. As I became more experienced, I began to see how rapidly the tools, languages, and methodologies I had learned early on could become obsolete. I had to stay agile, always open to learning new things, whether it was a new programming language, a different framework, or an entirely new way of approaching a problem. I realized that the best engineers are those who can adapt to change and embrace new tools without becoming too attached to the ones they've already mastered. It was during this phase that I truly understood the value of lifelong learning. It became clear that my technical skills were not finite but constantly evolving as long as I kept pushing myself to learn and grow.

Looking back, I can see that the evolution of my skills and mindset as a software engineer has been intertwined with my personal growth. The challenges I faced whether technical or interpersonal shaped not just the engineer I became, but the person I am today. I learned how to handle failure with grace, how to navigate the complexities of teamwork, and how to communicate technical ideas in a way that others could understand. But most importantly, I learned that the journey of becoming a great software engineer is never truly complete. It is an ongoing process of self-reflection, learning, and adaptation. There will always be new challenges, new technologies, and new opportunities to grow. What has changed over the years is my mindset from one of uncertainty and self-doubt to one of confidence, curiosity, and resilience.

As I continue to progress in my career, I remain mindful of the lessons I've learned and the growth I've experienced. I now know that being a great software engineer isn't about knowing everything; it's about having the mindset to keep learning, the humility to accept that there's always more to learn, and the perseverance to keep pushing through challenges. The skills I've developed over the years both technical, interpersonal, and strategic have all contributed to shaping who I am today. However, it's the evolution of my mindset that has truly been the driving force behind my growth. It has taught me that software engineering is as much about the journey as it is about the destination, and that with the right mindset, there is always more to discover.

Over the course of my career as a software engineer, the nature of tools, languages, and methodologies has undergone dramatic transformations. When I first started, many of the tools and practices that seemed cutting-edge then are now obsolete or have evolved into something far more sophisticated. This constant evolution is both one of the most exciting and daunting aspects of the field of software engineering. The pace of change in technology demands adaptability, a willingness to learn, and an openness to continuously rethinking the way we approach problems. Reflecting on the tools and methodologies I have encountered and adapted to over the years has given me a deep appreciation for the dynamic nature of the software engineering profession.

In the early stages of my career, the primary focus was on mastering specific languages and getting comfortable with a small set of tools. The technology landscape was far more static, and companies tended to stick to the same programming languages and frameworks for extended periods. I started my journey with languages like Java and C, focusing on building the foundational knowledge of how to write software that worked. These languages provided the structure and syntax I needed to understand programming logic, data structures, and algorithms. In many ways, they were the bedrock of my development. Back then, knowing how to work with a language was enough. My success was defined by how well I could solve problems using the tools I had at hand.

However, as my career progressed, it became clear that the real challenge was not simply knowing a language but understanding how to choose the right language or tool for the job. The more I learned, the more I realized that no one tool could address all of the challenges I encountered. I quickly moved from focusing solely on languages to embracing the broader ecosystem of tools available to software engineers. Early on, I was introduced to version control systems like

Git. The shift from local file systems to repositories with versioning was a game-changer. Git allowed for better collaboration, safer experimentation, and an overall improvement in the workflow. This was an exciting moment, as I began to see how the right tools could drastically improve productivity and the quality of the code I wrote.

As I continued my journey, the rise of new tools and technologies required me to be increasingly adaptable. The rapid development of web technologies played a significant role in this shift. In the early 2000s, the world of web development was much less mature than it is today. When I first ventured into web development, HTML and CSS were the primary tools for building user interfaces, and JavaScript was often considered a secondary language. However, the growth of JavaScript frameworks like Angular, React, and Vue.js transformed the way I thought about front-end development. These frameworks introduced new paradigms for building dynamic, responsive applications. With these tools, I could create richer user experiences that were previously only imaginable. Adapting to these technologies was a key turning point in my career. It taught me the importance of staying curious, exploring new frameworks, and finding solutions that fit the needs of the business.

The evolution of tools and languages wasn't confined to the front end. At the back end, the emergence of cloud computing and microservices introduced entirely new ways of designing and deploying applications. Early in my career, I worked with monolithic architectures where applications were built as a single, tightly coupled unit. While monolithic applications had their advantages in terms of simplicity, they also posed significant challenges as systems grew larger. As teams expanded, it became increasingly difficult to scale and manage these monolithic applications. I witnessed firsthand the rise of microservices, which allowed for greater flexibility in scaling individual components of an application without disrupting the entire system. The introduction of containerization technologies like Docker and container orchestration platforms like Kubernetes further transformed the landscape. These tools allowed for faster development cycles, easier testing, and greater portability. The shift toward cloud-native architectures and services also marked a major milestone in my career. I had to learn new cloud platforms, such as AWS and Azure, which offered managed services that could handle everything from databases to security to monitoring. Cloud platforms simplified much of the operational burden, enabling teams to focus on writing code rather than managing infrastructure.

At the same time, software development methodologies evolved rapidly, with Agile becoming the dominant approach. When I first started, software development was largely dominated by Waterfall methodologies which are long, structured development cycles where each phase had to be completed before the next one could begin. While Waterfall had its merits in certain contexts, it was often inefficient and inflexible in a fast-paced development environment. As the demand for quicker iterations and more flexible approaches increased, efficient methodologies began to take center stage.

Initially, the concept of agile was somewhat foreign to me. The idea of breaking down large projects into smaller, iterative chunks and constantly iterating based on feedback seemed like a significant departure from the traditional model. However, over time, I saw the immense benefits of this new approach. The ability to iterate quickly, focus on delivering value incrementally, and constantly refine the product based on user feedback became a crucial part of my work.

This new method also emphasized the importance of collaboration and communication within teams. The early stages of my career often involved isolated work where individual engineers would complete tasks without much interaction with others. However, as this approach became more widely adopted, it became clear that effective communication and collaboration were just as important as technical expertise. The importance of daily stand-ups, sprint planning, retrospectives, and pair programming became a core part of my work life. I learned to communicate more effectively with stakeholders, to engage in regular feedback loops, and to work collaboratively to solve problems. This shift in methodology wasn't just about adopting new tools; it was about changing the mindset of how we approach software development as a whole.

The rise of Continuous Integration and Continuous Deployment (CI/CD) tools also played a critical role in reshaping the way software was developed and deployed. In the past, the process of integrating new code into a project was often cumbersome and error-prone, leading to long release cycles and a higher risk of bugs slipping through. The introduction of CI/CD pipelines allowed for automated testing, building, and deployment, greatly reducing the friction of releasing new features and updates. The implementation of CI/CD became a crucial practice in my own development process. It provided a more streamlined, efficient approach to delivering code to production, and it also helped catch issues earlier in the development process. This evolution towards automation has not only made the process of shipping software more efficient but also allowed for greater reliability and stability in production environments.

Having reflection on the tools and methodologies that have come and gone throughout my career, I realize that they are not just isolated components of my technical journey, but they represent the broader evolution of the industry itself. Technologies like Git, cloud computing, microservices, and CI/CD are emblematic of how software engineering is increasingly becoming about collaboration, scalability, and automation. In the early days of my career, development was very much about solving technical problems at an individual level. Today, software engineering is a more collaborative, multidisciplinary field that demands a broader skill set such as one that blends technical expertise with an understanding of business needs, team dynamics, and user experience.

Perhaps the most striking aspect of my career's evolution has been learning to embrace change. In the beginning, I often felt that a tool or technology was something to master, and once I mastered it, I could rely on it for years to come. Over time, I've learned that technology is always evolving, and the best engineers are those who can adapt and embrace new tools, languages, and methodologies as they emerge. What I learned about the tools I used in the past wasn't just about their immediate usefulness, but it was about understanding the underlying principles that made them effective and applying those principles to new tools and technologies.

As I continue to work in the software industry, I find that keeping up with emerging technologies is not just a matter of adding new tools to my skill set but involves understanding how these tools fit into the larger ecosystem and how they align with the needs of the business. Tools and methodologies will continue to evolve, and new ones will emerge, but the core skills of software engineers such as problem-solving, collaboration, and continuous learning will remain constant. My journey with tools and methodologies has been one of adaptation, but it has also been one of recognition. I've learned to appreciate that the tools we use in software development are ultimately just that, tools. What matters most is how we use them to solve problems, deliver value, and improve the way we work.

The concept of lifelong learning has been central to my journey as a software engineer. The nature of our field demands it as technology evolves rapidly, methodologies change, and new challenges emerge constantly. Looking back on my career, the importance of maintaining a growth mindset, the constant pursuit of knowledge, and the need to remain adaptable have been key to my success. Software engineering is not a static profession where one can simply "arrive" at mastery and stop learning. Instead, it is a field in perpetual motion, where the tools and techniques of today may be obsolete tomorrow. This continuous cycle of learning has not only shaped the technical aspects of my work but has also influenced my personal growth, my ability to lead others, and my approach to solving problems.

Now when I started my early professional days, I was aware that becoming a proficient software engineer required more than just completing a coding bootcamp or obtaining a degree in computer science. While these credentials helped me get my foot in the door, the real learning began once I started working on real and everyday projects. The skills required in practice were far more nuanced and complex than those presented in textbooks or tutorials. At first, I focused on mastering the basics: learning languages, understanding algorithms, and becoming familiar with the most commonly used frameworks and libraries. But as I progressed, I realized that the true essence of software engineering lay not in knowing the specifics of any one technology but in cultivating a mindset that allowed me to thrive in the face of uncertainty and complexity.

The first step in embracing lifelong learning was acknowledging that I didn't know everything. It was easy to fall into the trap of thinking that I needed to know every programming language, every tool, and every design pattern in order to be successful. But over time, I learned that the most successful engineers are those who are humble enough to admit that there is always more to learn. This mindset shift was liberating. It allowed me to embrace new challenges without fear of failure and to approach every project as an opportunity for growth rather than simply a task to complete. I stopped worrying about whether I had all the answers and started focusing on how to find them.

As software engineering has become more complex, it has become increasingly important to learn how to learn. Early in my career, I relied heavily on tutorials, books, and courses to expand my knowledge. While these resources were invaluable, they only took me so far. At some point, I had to shift from passive learning to active learning by actively seeking out opportunities to apply my knowledge and engage with the broader engineering community. Conferences, meetups, and online forums became essential for keeping up with industry trends and for learning from others who had faced similar challenges. I found that the more I engaged with the community, the more I learned not just about the latest tools and technologies but also about different ways of thinking and solving problems. Collaborating with engineers from diverse backgrounds and experiences opened my eyes to new perspectives and methodologies that I could incorporate into my own work.

Beyond formal learning and engagement with the community, I also began to focus on experiential learning. In the early days of my career, I would often find myself stuck on a problem for hours, only to realize that the solution was relatively simple. This was a frustrating but ultimately valuable experience because it taught me how to approach problems systematically and how to learn from mistakes. I started to view every challenge as an opportunity to learn, whether it was a bug in the code or a design flaw in an architecture. I realized that every failure was a lesson in disguise. By reflecting on what went wrong and how I could improve, I began to see my mistakes as steppingstones toward mastery rather than setbacks. This mindset of learning from failure became an essential part of my professional development.

The importance of mentorship played a significant role in my learning journey as well. Both as a mentee and a mentor, I have experienced firsthand the value of sharing knowledge and learning from others. As a junior developer, I was fortunate to have mentors who guided me through the intricacies of software development. They taught me not just the technical skills I needed but also the soft skills but how to communicate effectively, how to collaborate with others, and how to think critically about software design. Having someone to ask questions, share frustrations with, and receive feedback from was invaluable in accelerating my growth. Over time, I also took on mentoring roles myself. Teaching others not only reinforced my own knowledge but also challenged me to think more deeply about the concepts I was teaching. It became clear that mentorship was not just about passing on knowledge but about learning together. Every mentoring relationship was an opportunity to grow, both as a teacher and as a learner.

In addition to the value of mentorship, I learned that the most effective software engineers are those who embrace interdisciplinary learning. The world of software engineering is vast, and the challenges we face rarely fit neatly into a single domain. Over the years, I found myself working in different areas of the software stack: front-end, back-end, databases, and even DevOps. Each of these areas required a different set of skills and knowledge, and I had to be adaptable enough to learn and master each new domain. This kind of breadth, however, was not enough on its own. As I gained experience, I realized the importance of depth in certain areas, especially those that aligned with my interests and the needs of the teams I worked with. By combining breadth with depth, I was able to become a more well-rounded engineer, able to approach complex problems from multiple angles and bring a more holistic perspective to my work.

One of the most important lessons I've learned in my journey of lifelong learning is the need to stay adaptable. The world of software engineering is characterized by rapid change, and the tools, languages, and frameworks we use today may not be relevant in the years to come. When I first started, the focus was on learning languages like Java and C++, but now, there is an increasing emphasis on languages like Python, JavaScript, and Go. The rise of cloud computing, machine learning, and artificial intelligence has further complicated the landscape, introducing a whole new set of skills that engineers must master in order to remain relevant. For a long time, I focused on becoming highly proficient in a few specific areas. But as I progressed in my career, I realized that flexibility was just as important as expertise. To stay relevant in a rapidly changing field, I had to be willing to step outside my comfort zone, learn new technologies, and adapt to shifting industry demands.

The pace of technological change is not only driven by new programming languages or frameworks but also by the increasing complexity of systems we build. As software systems have become more interconnected and distributed, the challenge of maintaining and scaling applications has grown. No longer is it enough to write code that works in isolation; we must now think about how our code interacts with other systems, how it scales, how it handles failure, and how it meets the needs of the business. To navigate this complexity, engineers must not only be technically proficient but also have a deep understanding of the broader system architecture. This is why the concept of lifelong learning extends beyond just acquiring new tools— it also involves learning how to manage complexity, how to think in systems, and how to anticipate future needs.

As I reflect on my journey, it becomes clear that lifelong learning is not a destination but a process. The tools and technologies we use today will inevitably evolve, and new challenges will continue to emerge. The most successful engineers are those who maintain a growth mindset, who are curious, and who are not afraid to learn new things even if that means stepping outside their comfort zones. I've learned that the key to thriving in this field is not just about acquiring technical knowledge but about cultivating the ability to adapt, innovate, and collaborate with others. Lifelong learning has shaped who I am as a software engineer and continues to drive my passion for the craft. As

I look ahead, I know that the journey of learning and growing will never truly end, and that's what makes the field of software engineering so exciting.

I would also love to point out that there are areas, some already touched in facets during the course of this book, and some notes that you should reflect on as you evolve in your mindset, skills and tools as a software engineer aiming for the stars.

The influence of technology on modern society is profound, shaping how we communicate, work, learn, and even think. As the creators of this technology, those involved in its design and implementation carry a weighty responsibility. This responsibility extends beyond technical proficiency to encompass the ethical implications of their work. Navigating this landscape requires a deep commitment to understanding the broader consequences of decisions and ensuring that the products and systems created serve humanity in equitable and just ways.

Ethics in technology begins with intentionality. At its core lies a simple yet powerful question: What impact will this have? This question, when asked at every stage of development, can transform how projects are approached and executed. It shifts the focus from merely meeting specifications or deadlines to understanding the ripple effects of every decision. For instance, developing an algorithm that prioritizes efficiency may unintentionally marginalize certain user groups. Recognizing this possibility early and striving for inclusiveness not only improves the technology but also ensures that it serves a diverse population fairly.

However, the answers to ethical questions are rarely straightforward. Technology often operates in gray areas, where innovation and accountability must coexist. A product designed with good intentions might still have unintended consequences. Consider the rise of artificial intelligence in decision-making processes. While AI can improve efficiency and reduce human error, it can also perpetuate biases embedded in its training data. The challenge is not just identifying these risks but actively working to mitigate them, even when it requires additional effort or resources.

One of the most compelling examples of ethical responsibility lies in data privacy. The collection and use of data have become central to modern systems, yet this convenience often comes at the expense of individual autonomy. Balancing the benefits of data-driven insights with the right to privacy demands a nuanced approach. Transparency becomes essential as users must understand how their data is used and have the ability to make informed choices. Engineers who prioritize privacy as a fundamental right, rather than an afterthought, set a standard that others can follow.

Beyond privacy, accessibility represents another critical ethical dimension. Technology should empower everyone, regardless of their abilities or circumstances. Designing for inclusivity means considering the needs of people with disabilities, those in underserved communities, or individuals with limited access to resources. This might involve creating interfaces that are screen-reader friendly, optimizing apps for low-bandwidth environments, or supporting multiple languages. Small decisions, such as ensuring proper contrast in a user interface or providing captions for videos, can make a significant difference in someone's experience.

Ethics is not only about the products created but also the processes followed during their development. Transparency and accountability should be cornerstones of every project. Teams must foster a culture where ethical concerns are raised and addressed without fear of reprisal. Encouraging open discussions about potential risks, trade-offs, and societal impacts helps ensure that decisions are well-informed and balanced. Leadership plays a crucial role in setting this tone, demonstrating that ethical considerations are not optional but integral to the success of any endeavor.

As technology keeps changing, so too must the ethical frameworks be guiding its development. Staying informed about emerging issues such as the environmental costs of computing, the ethics of autonomous systems, or the implications of genetic data requires ongoing education and dialogue. Engaging with these topics is not a burden but a privilege, offering an opportunity to shape the future in meaningful ways. It also fosters a sense of purpose, reminding those in the field that their work has relevant and world implications. Ethical challenges also extend beyond the individual to the collective. Collaborating with peers to establish industry-wide standards can amplify positive impact. Initiatives like open-source ethics guidelines, inclusive design principles, and community-driven audits of algorithms demonstrate how collective action can address systemic issues. These efforts show that ethics is not a solitary pursuit but a shared responsibility.

Personal values play a vital role in navigating ethical dilemmas. Aligning professional decisions with a strong moral compass creates clarity and consistency, even in complex situations. This alignment often requires courage and standing firm in the face of pressure to prioritize profits over principles or speed over safety. Yet, making ethical choices, even when difficult, reinforces integrity and sets a powerful example for others. Fundamentally, ethics in technology is about striving for a balance between innovation and responsibility. It's about ensuring that the benefits of progress are shared equitably, that risks are minimized, and that the rights and dignity of all people are upheld. This requires more than technical expertise; it demands empathy, foresight, and a willingness to question assumptions. By embracing this challenge, those involved in creating technology not only build better systems but also contribute to a better world.

Ethics may not always provide clear answers, but it does provide a framework for asking the right questions. What values guide your decisions? How will your work impact others, both today and in the future? Are you willing to take a stand when it matters most? These questions are not merely theoretical, but they define the legacy of every project and every career. Answering them with honesty and humility ensures that the pursuit of technological advancement remains grounded in the service of humanity.

A second vital area is how refined are your soft communication skills. Technical expertise may form the backbone of a successful career in the technology industry, but soft skills are the connective tissue that hold everything together. For too long, these non-technical abilities such as communication, empathy, collaboration, and adaptability have been viewed as secondary to technical prowess. Yet, the reality is that they play a crucial and often underappreciated role in shaping the success of individuals and teams alike. Mastering these skills is not just a complement to technical knowledge; it is an essential part of excelling in any professional setting.

At the heart of effective collaboration lies the ability to communicate clearly and meaningfully. The brilliance of a technical solution can be completely undermined if it cannot be conveyed in a way that resonates with others. Whether discussing project requirements with stakeholders, explaining design decisions to a team, or presenting findings to non-technical audiences, the way ideas are articulated matters. Clarity ensures alignment, reduces misunderstandings, and builds trust. It also empowers teams to work toward a shared goal without unnecessary friction.

The challenge with communication in technology is its inherently interdisciplinary nature. Developers, designers, project managers, and executives each bring their own perspectives, priorities, and terminologies. Bridging these gaps requires more than technical accuracy; it demands empathy and the ability to see things from another's point of view. For instance, while engineers might focus on system performance, stakeholders may prioritize user experience or market viability. Recognizing and addressing these differing concerns not only facilitates better collaboration but also leads to more holistic solutions.

Listening is a key component of this process. Too often, conversations become one-sided, with individuals focused on conveying their own ideas rather than genuinely engaging with others. Active listening fosters understanding, helping to uncover hidden concerns or insights that might otherwise be overlooked. It also demonstrates respect, showing colleagues and stakeholders that their perspectives are valued. This simple act can transform relationships, creating an environment where ideas flow freely, and innovation thrives. Another critical aspect of communication is storytelling. While data and logic are foundational to any technical argument, it is stories that connect with people on a deeper level. Crafting a compelling narrative around a project or idea can make it more relatable and memorable. For example, rather than presenting a new feature purely in terms of its functionality, framing it as a solution to a user's pain point or a way to enhance their experience can resonate more strongly. Storytelling humanizes technical work, making it accessible and impactful.

Empathy, while often associated with interpersonal relationships, is just as vital in the context of user-centered design and problem-solving. Understanding the needs, challenges, and perspectives of end-users enables the creation of systems and applications that truly serve their intended purpose. This extends beyond designing for convenience or aesthetics; it means anticipating how users will interact with technology, identifying potential barriers, and striving to make solutions inclusive and accessible to all.

Beyond users, empathy is equally important within teams. The fast-paced nature of the industry can sometimes lead to high-pressure situations, disagreements, or miscommunications. In such moments, taking the time to understand the motivations and emotions of colleagues can prevent conflicts from escalating and strengthen relationships. A team that operates with empathy is better equipped to navigate challenges and adapt to change, fostering a culture of mutual support and resilience.

Collaboration, of course, is where many soft skills converge. It is not enough to simply work alongside others; true collaboration involves leveraging the strengths of each team member to achieve a collective goal. This requires humility, recognizing that no one person has all the answers and a willingness to learn from others. It also involves balancing assertiveness with openness, advocating for your ideas while remaining receptive to feedback and alternative perspectives. Adaptability is another cornerstone of soft skills in technology. The field evolves rapidly, and with it, the skills, tools, and methodologies required to stay relevant. But adaptability is not limited to technical learning; it also encompasses the ability to navigate organizational changes, shifting priorities, and unforeseen challenges. This flexibility enables individuals to remain effective even in uncertain or unfamiliar situations, turning potential setbacks into opportunities for growth.

Time and again, the importance of these skills becomes evident in the workplace. Consider a situation where a critical project is delayed due to unforeseen technical issues. While technical expertise is essential to resolve the problem, it is soft skills that determine how effectively the situation is managed. Communicating the delay transparently to stakeholders, collaborating with the team to devise a solution, and maintaining morale during a stressful period require a combination of emotional intelligence, communication, and leadership.

Moreover, soft skills play a pivotal role in personal development and career progression. Technical knowledge can open doors, but it is soft skills that often determine how far someone can go. They shape how individuals are perceived by colleagues, managers, and clients, influencing opportunities for mentorship, leadership, and collaboration. They also contribute to building a reputation for reliability, professionalism, and approachability, which are qualities that are as valuable as technical acumen. Cultivating these skills is a lifelong process, one that requires intention and effort. Unlike technical knowledge, which can often be acquired through formal education or practice, soft skills are deeply rooted in self-awareness and interpersonal experiences. Reflecting on your own communication style, seeking feedback from others, and embracing opportunities to work with diverse teams are all ways to strengthen these abilities.

In the end, the true measure of success is not just what is built, but how it is built. The technical brilliance of a project may earn accolades, but it is the thoughtfulness, inclusivity, and humanity behind it that leave a lasting impact. Soft skills are the bridge between technical expertise and real-world relevance, enabling individuals to navigate complexities, inspire teams, and create technology that truly matters. Embracing and honing these skills unlocks the full potential of not just the work itself, but the people behind it.

The place of deep self reflection and leaving strides for others to follow and achieve greater feats hold a special place in my heart as an evolution every professional and individual should endeavor to pass through. The concept of legacy often feels distant, something to be considered only at the twilight of a career. Yet, the truth is that every action, decision, and interaction contributes to the legacy we leave behind. In the world of technology, where the pace of change can make yesterday's innovations obsolete, legacy is less about the tools and systems we build and more about the impact we have on people and the values we champion. Legacy is not just about what we create but it is about how we make others feel, what we inspire in them, and how we influence the culture of the spaces we inhabit.

Leaving a legacy begins with intention. What do you want to stand for? This question, while simple, requires deep introspection. It asks you to consider the principles that guide your work, the causes you care about, and the ways in which you wish to be remembered. Some might aim to push the boundaries of innovation, while others focus on fostering inclusive environments or mentoring the next generation. Whatever the focus, clarity about your purpose lays the foundation for building a meaningful legacy.

Legacy is often most evident in relationships. The connections forged with colleagues, mentees, and collaborators are the threads that weave a career into something greater than the sum of its parts. Investing time and energy into these relationships has a ripple effect. A moment spent mentoring a junior developer, offering a listening ear during a difficult time, or celebrating a team member's success may seem small, but these acts create lasting impressions. People remember not only what you did but how you made them feel. Being approachable, supportive, and kind leaves a mark that transcends the workplace. For many, legacy is also tied to the culture they help shape. Culture is not defined by a single individual but by the collective actions and attitudes of everyone in a team or organization. However, individuals have the power to influence culture in meaningful ways. Demonstrating integrity, advocating for fairness, and promoting collaboration set a tone that others often follow. Whether it's championing diversity, encouraging open communication, or fostering a culture of continuous learning, the values you embody contribute to the broader environment and inspire those around you.

One of the most enduring aspects of legacy is the knowledge shared, and the lessons imparted. In a field driven by constant learning and adaptation, the insights and wisdom passed on to others become invaluable. Writing documentation, sharing experiences through blogs or talks, and mentoring peers or newcomers are all ways of ensuring that your knowledge continues to make an impact even after you've moved on. Every time someone builds upon something you've taught or takes inspiration from your work, they become part of your legacy.

However, it is not only about successes; it also encompasses how we navigate failures. A willingness to admit mistakes, learn from them, and share those lessons openly can have a profound effect on those around us. It shows that vulnerability and growth are not weaknesses but strengths. By normalizing failure as part of the journey, you create an environment where others feel safe to take risks and innovate. This mindset shift is a powerful contribution to the culture and people you leave behind.

Legacy also extends to the systems and processes established during your tenure. While the specific technologies may evolve or be replaced, the ways in which problems are approached, and solutions are implemented often endure. Creating efficient workflows, advocating for ethical practices, and embedding principles of sustainability into projects are all ways of influencing the future long after your direct involvement has ended. These contributions might not always be visible, but their impact shapes the experiences of those who come after.

Perhaps one of the most overlooked yet profound aspects of legacy is the inspiration you provide. By leading with passion and purpose, you spark the same in others. Seeing someone deeply committed to their craft, whether through their technical expertise, their dedication to fostering teamwork, or their advocacy for social responsibility, is contagious. It motivates others to strive for excellence, to push boundaries, and to reflect on their own aspirations. This inspiration often spreads far beyond immediate circles, touching people you may never meet. Legacy, however, is not a static endpoint; it evolves over time. What begins as a personal aspiration grows and changes as you move through different roles, work with diverse teams, and encounter new challenges. There's beauty in this evolution. It reflects the dynamic nature of both personal growth and the ever-changing world of technology. A legacy built on adaptability, curiosity, and an openness to change becomes timeless, resonating with people regardless of the specific context or era.

It's also important to acknowledge that it is not something you control entirely. While you can shape your actions and influence those around you, how others interpret and carry forward your contributions is beyond your reach. This is not a limitation but a testament to the power of collective memory and collaboration. It is not about individual recognition, but it is about the shared impact created by and for others. It is a partnership, a co-creation that spans time and space.

The measure of a meaningful legacy is not the accolades received, or the lines of code written but the lives touched. It is in the stories people tell about how you made them think differently, how you supported them during a challenging time, or how your work inspired them to take a leap of faith. It is in the culture you helped build, the knowledge you passed on, and the values you upheld. It is in the countless small moments that, together, form a lasting impression.

Building a legacy is not about perfection. It is about authenticity, consistency, and a commitment to contributing something positive to the world around you. By approaching every interaction, decision, and challenge with these principles in mind, you create a legacy that is not just remembered but felt. It becomes a source of inspiration and guidance for others, a beacon that continues to shine long after you've moved on.

All these and more define a holistic, sustainable and impactful evolution of not just a software engineer but any individuals seeking to make impact on and off their professional platforms.

FINAL THOUGHTS

As I am near the end of sharing my experiences and lessons learned throughout my career, I want to take a moment to reflect not only on what I've learned but on how you, as a reader, might apply these insights to your own professional journey. The story I've shared is one of growth, adaptation, and learning. But it is by no means a one-size-fits-all narrative. My path has been shaped by the unique challenges and opportunities I've faced, the choices I've made, and the lessons I've absorbed. However, the overarching message of this book isn't to present a blueprint that you must follow; rather, it is to offer a compass, a tool for you to navigate your own journey with intention, curiosity, and resilience.

What's important to understand is that every career is a personal story, and there is no single path to success. The tech industry, and every other field for that matter, is vast and filled with countless opportunities, challenges, and evolving circumstances. While the lessons I've shared may resonate with you, they are grounded in my own experiences and perceptions. What I have learned is deeply influenced by the environment I've worked in, the colleagues I've collaborated with, and the mistakes I've made along the way. Your own journey will be shaped by different factors which could be your values, the industry you work in, the people you interact with, and even the unique challenges you encounter along the way.

In reflecting on my career and offering these lessons, I want to emphasize the importance of flexibility. The ability to adapt to changing circumstances has been one of the defining features of my career. What worked yesterday may not be the right solution for today, and what works today may become obsolete tomorrow. This is especially true in fast-moving industries like technology, but the same principle holds true across many sectors. Whether you're in healthcare, finance, education, or the arts, the ability to stay flexible, to continuously reassess your goals, and to shift your approach as new information emerges will serve you well in the long run.

One of the most profound realizations I've had throughout my career is that professional growth is often nonlinear. In the early years, we're taught to climb the ladder, to seek promotions, titles, and bigger projects. But I've come to understand that growth isn't always about moving up. Sometimes, growth means moving sideways, expanding your skill set, or even stepping back to reassess what truly matters to you. Many times, growth is less about measurable milestones and more about the quiet evolution that happens as you learn, reflect, and adapt. It's about developing new skills, cultivating wisdom, and gaining the perspective necessary to make better decisions. There have been times in my career when I felt I was stagnant, or even moving backward, only to realize that those periods of "stasis" were laying the foundation for deeper, more meaningful progress.

As you read my story and reflect on your own, it's important to remember that success is subjective. We are often conditioned to think of success in terms of titles, paychecks, and outward validation. However, true success is far more personal and nuanced. Success is about alignment such as aligning your work with your values, your goals, and your deeper sense of purpose. It's about feeling fulfilled in the work you do, whether or not that work comes with a prestigious title or a large paycheck. It's also about knowing when to say no, whether that means rejecting a project that doesn't align with your values or turning down opportunities that would push you further from the life balance you want. These decisions, while sometimes difficult, are often the most powerful ones you can make in your career. Trusting yourself and having the courage to carve out your own path is an essential part of professional fulfillment.

The collective power of a well-functioning team, the ability to learn from each other, and the willingness to share ideas is what allows individuals to grow and, ultimately, produce exceptional work. My success has never been the result of my efforts alone; it has always been shaped by the teams I've worked with and the mentors who have guided me.

But the value of community extends beyond just work. I've come to appreciate the importance of surrounding yourself with people who inspire and challenge you, not just in terms of professional skills, but in terms of mindset, values, and perspectives. The people I admire most in my career are not necessarily the ones who have the most impressive resumes but the ones who are committed to personal growth, who challenge the status quo, and who encourage those around them to strive for more. Building a network of people who support you, who push you to think differently, and who help you stay grounded is invaluable. These relationships are not just career assets; they are sources of personal growth and resilience. In the face of adversity, it's often the relationships you have built that will carry you through the toughest times.

The path to success is rarely a straight line, and setbacks are inevitable. Whether it's a failed project, a missed promotion, or an industry shift that forces you to change direction, challenges are a natural part of the journey. Early in my career, I found myself frustrated by these setbacks, wondering if I had made the wrong choices or if I wasn't cut out for certain roles. But with time, I realized that setbacks were simply part of the learning process. The most successful people I know are not those who avoid failure but those who learn from it, adapt, and keep going. Understanding your own strengths, weaknesses, and limitations allows you to make better decisions and navigate the complexities of professional life. One of the most important lessons I've learned is that no one succeeds in a vacuum. We all need help from others whether it's through mentorship, collaboration, or simply seeking advice. Acknowledging that you don't have all the answers and being open to learning from others is not a weakness but a strength. As a leader, I learned that vulnerability and the willingness to admit when I don't know something can actually be a powerful tool. It fosters trust and openness, creating an environment where others feel comfortable sharing their own insights and challenges.

Finally, as you reflect on your own journey, I encourage you to think about the kind of legacy you want to leave behind. In the early stages of my career, I focused primarily on immediate success, building my skill set, gaining experience, and climbing the proverbial ladder. Over time, however, I've come to realize that the impact you have on others is just as important as the work you produce. The legacy we leave is often shaped by how we treat others, how we share our knowledge, and how we empower those who come after us. Your legacy doesn't have to be grand or widely recognized, but it should be meaningful. Whether it's through mentoring others, contributing to the community, or simply being someone who encourages and uplifts others, the impact you have on people is what will endure.

As you embark on your own journey, remember that it's not about following a set of rigid rules or adopting a single perspective. My career has been shaped by my own unique experiences, challenges, and choices and your journey will be just as unique. Use the lessons I've shared as a guide but know that they are not prescriptions.

Rather, they are reflections from my journey, insights that may offer direction, but ultimately, you must forge your own path. Stay curious, stay humble, and stay adaptable. Your career is a marathon, not a sprint, and the most important thing is to keep moving forward with intention, passion, and the willingness to grow.

ABOUT THE AUTHOR

Iyiola Ladejo is an expert software engineer with over a decade of experience in the tech industry. Passionate about innovation, problem-solving, and the power of technology to shape the future, Iyiola has honed his skills across a variety of sectors, contributing to numerous successful projects and leading high-performance teams. A dedicated lifelong learner, he believes in the importance of continuous growth, both professionally and personally. Through mentorship and collaboration, he has influenced the careers of many aspiring engineers. When he's not coding, Iyiola is an avid advocate for teaching and community-building in the tech world and beyond, helping others navigate their own journeys in their respective fields.

www.ingramcontent.com/pod-product-compliance
Lightning Source LLC
LaVergne TN
LVHW091458170726
843492LV00001B/246